The Sustainability Handbook
for Design and Technology Teachers

The Sustainability Handbook has been produced by Practical Action in collaboration with the Centre for Alternative Technology and Loughborough University. Funded by the European Community and the Countryside Council for Wales. The contents of this publication are the sole responsibility of Practical Action and can in no way be taken to reflect the views of the European Union.

Practical Action, The Schumacher Centre, Bourton on Dunsmore, Rugby, Warwickshire CV23 9QZ
Centre for Alternative Technology, Machynlleth, Powys SY20 9AZ
ISBN 978 1 85339 670 0
© Practical Action and Centre for Alternative Technology, 2008
Reprinted 2009, 2010, 2011

Contents

(A) = Activity

Introduction

Ready for sustainability?

We want the world to be a great, sustainable place to live in – for ourselves, for people living in all other countries, and for future generations.

This pack is about a more sustainable world, and how Design and Technology teachers and students can contribute to it.

We hope that a greater understanding of sustainability issues will enable D&T teachers and students to understand that:

- a sustainable world is an exciting, interesting and hopeful place to live in
- young people can be at the forefront of making the world a better place
- sustainable schools can exemplify a sustainable way of life.

Every product that's around us is designed by somebody – and design decisions are based on values. This pack will enable students to produce great designs and great products based on sustainability principles. They will understand that:

- designing and making beautiful, durable products that people want to keep and treasure minimises negative impacts
- climate change results from lifestyle choices and has major social, economic and environmental impacts
- the effects of climate change can be reduced by making informed decisions on energy use and material choice
- biodiversity is vital for a sustainable future, and lack of it threatens health, food security and economic stability
- all products have some negative impacts, including those that are natural or recycled.

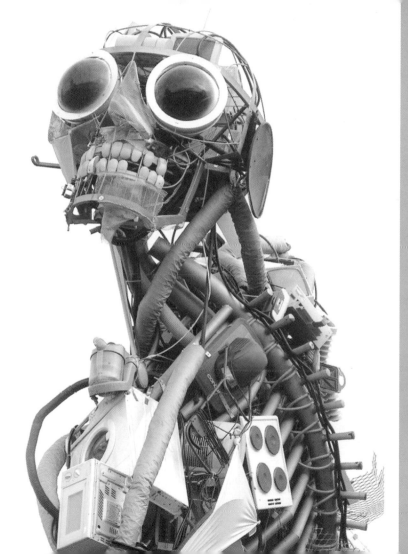

Using activities from this pack, students will also learn that we can care for our world by:

- being careful with the world's resources, which have to be shared among 6.4 billion people

- ensuring we don't use up the resources of future generations

- taking the trouble to find out the potential effects of our designs on the environment

- designing in a way that has positive effects for everyone in the world, not just a privileged few.

BIG ISSUES

SUSTAINABLE DESIGN
The big issues

Why is sustainable design important?

If everyone in the world lived as we do in the UK now, we would need three planets to sustain us

Over-consumption

Britain throws away £20 billion worth of unused food every year – equal to five times our spending on international aid and enough to lift 150 million people out of starvation. (*The Independent* 15.03.05)

Wasteful energy use

It takes 5 kilowatt-hours of energy to turn wood into a thick glossy magazine like *Seventeen.* That's enough energy to run a low-energy lamp for at least 250 hours. Mobile phone chargers left plugged in cost £60m per annum and produce 250,000 tonnes of CO_2. (www.guardian.co.uk)

Design for short life

The average lifespan of a computer in developed countries is 2 years. In Europe people keep a mobile phone for 18 months on average. (UNEP Vital Graphics)

But what if we designed like this...?

Brompton bike
– makes it easy
to use public
transport for longer
journeys. Rides almost like a large-wheel bike.
Folds quickly. And it's elegant.

MP3 player
– music using much
less material than CDs,
tapes or records and players.
But how long will you keep it?

Clothing from Howies – made
to last, ethically produced,
promotes local, outdoor
fun. And stylish.

No-Shank toothbrush –
minimising our use of materials.

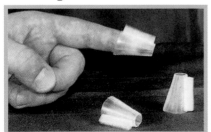

For more information visit:

www.myfootprint.org
(How big is your footprint?)

Climate change and sustainable design

Should we change the way we design?

Climate change is now accepted as the biggest threat to all people as well as other species on the planet (www.climatechallenge.gov.uk/communicate.html). But most people, including designers and makers, are not changing their behaviour. They aren't sure how it affects them and think it's a problem for the future.

Facts

- Human activity is having a huge impact on changing climates NOW.

- The effects are being felt far more in developing countries in Asia, Africa and Latin America. Many countries are already experiencing prolonged flooding or drought.

- There will be impacts in Europe within our lifetime – low fish stocks, rising sea levels, forest fires, crop failures, flooding, lack of snow, heat and cold-related deaths.

- Its causes are more often brought about by developed countries like the UK – the average Briton produces 126 times more CO_2 than a Nepali (Tyndall Centre).

- Even if we cut CO_2 emissions by 50% this century the temperature will still increase by 4-5°C.

- The 'average' African is still using less energy than the 'average' person used in England in 1875 (Christian Aid).

- 'There is still time to avoid the worst impacts of climate change if we take strong action now.' (Stern Review, 2006)

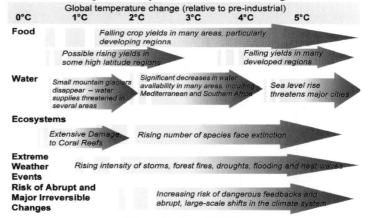

Projected Impacts of Climate Change

Global temperature change (relative to pre-industrial)

| 0°C | 1°C | 2°C | 3°C | 4°C | 5°C |

Food
- Falling crop yields in many areas, particularly developing regions
- Possible rising yields in some high latitude regions
- Falling yields in many developed regions

Water
- Small mountain glaciers disappear – water supplies threatened in several areas
- Significant decreases in water availability in many areas, including Mediterranean and Southern Africa
- Sea level rise threatens major cities

Ecosystems
- Extensive Damage to Coral Reefs
- Rising number of species face extinction

Extreme Weather Events
- Rising intensity of storms, forest fires, droughts, flooding and heat waves

Risk of Abrupt and Major Irreversible Changes
- Increasing risk of dangerous feedbacks and abrupt, large-scale shifts in the climate system

(Stern Review, 2006)

Make me desirable

Implications for good design

• Ask students to work in small groups to look at the chart opposite and brainstorm what direct and indirect effects a temperature rise of 5°C would have for them

• Report back from groups and discuss how these effects might change the role of designers. How might the idea of what is 'good design' need to alter? (www.climate challenge.gov.uk/communicate.html)

Implications for our lifestyles

• Ask students to work in pairs to look at http://carbongym.cat.org.uk/carbongym/ Go to calculate me.

• Work out the CO2 emissions of their current lifestyles through energy in the home, transport and food. Look at how this compares with the UK average and the global fair share.

• Discuss how they could reduce their individual carbon emissions.

Make me take action

Technology can help

Many charities are working to tackle climate change by enabling people to use technologies (e.g. Renewable energy) that contribute far less to climate change.

For example, tens of thousands of homes in Britain now have solar water heating systems on their roof, reducing by at least a half the amount of fossil fuels used to heat water for use in those homes.

To find out more about how people are developing technologies to reduce climate change here visit www.cat.org.uk www.energysavingtrust.org.uk/ Find out more about the technologies that are helping people most affected by climate change at www.practicalaction.org/id?= climatechange_background

Suitable for all D&T areas

Sustainable schools doorways

8

For more information visit:
www.stepin.org
www.informationinspiration.org.uk

Climate change – got the message?

How can people be persuaded to take climate change seriously?

Climate change is recognised as a huge problem – but human behaviour is slow to change. How can graphic designers communicate the messages of climate change? Making people feel guilty, or trying to make them think about their children's future, doesn't seem to work.

Discuss the following

- Environmentally, change is already clear - extreme weather (floods, heat waves, hurricanes), melting ice caps, rising sea levels.

- Access to water and food will be more difficult in many countries, which is likely to increase conflict.

- Tourism will be affected - the Mediterranean may be too hot, ski resorts may have no snow.

- It has been estimated that global Gross Domestic Product will fall by 5% each year if we don't act now. (Sir Nicholas Stern)

- In contrast, the costs of action to reduce greenhouse gas emissions could be limited to 1% of GDP each year. (Stern)

Got the message?

- Evaluate some of the graphics used in existing campaigns on climate change - see the links below. Do humour or sharp cartoons help to make people change?

- Design a campaign to get the people around you to take action on climate change. This could be posters, badges, T-shirts, word of mouth, an action - whatever you think will work.

Graphics

For more information visit:

www.climatechange.wmnet.org.uk/??.cfm

www.icount.org.uk/

www.peopleandplanet.org/

www.woodcraft.org.uk/projects/

www.grinningplanet.com/5005/environmental-jokes-cartoons.htm

Sustainable design and poverty

What's poverty got to do with D&T?

The choices we make as consumers and as designer-makers always have results for other people, both in our country and elsewhere in the world. If we buy flowers grown in Kenya, there are consequences for Kenyan flower-growers, their families, transport companies etc., and British flower growers and distributors may feel the effects of decreased demand for their product. Every decision we make as consumers, designers and manufacturers is likely to involve a moral dilemma.

This activity is designed to help students think about whether or not designers in developed countries like ours have a responsibility towards those living in countries that are less developed, sometimes in extreme poverty. It is open-ended, without suggesting answers. It is designed to encourage students to think about the results of their design decisions.

(Centre for Alternative Technology)

Activity - Belief circle

Organise your class into a circle. Ask each student to write his or her name boldly on a piece of reused paper.

Explain that you are going to put a statement on a piece of paper in the middle of the circle. Tell them they will have a short time to think about whether or not they agree or disagree with the statement. Tell them that when you ask them to do so, but not before, they should put their name paper as near to or as far away from the statement as their belief is near to or far away from the statement. So, if they strongly agree with the statement, `All designers have a responsibility to design for reducing climate change', they put their name paper adjacent to the statement. If they strongly disagree, they put their paper close to themselves.

When everyone has put their paper down, ask one person to explain their position and then open up discussion by asking others with different positions.

Suggested statements:

- It is always best to use local products or materials in our designs.

- My designing and making decisions here don't make any difference to people living in Africa.

- There's poverty in every country. As a designer I want to look after my own poor first.

- Making a product well is the most important task for a designer. For me, what is used and where it comes from are secondary concerns.

- It's not designers that exploit poor people, it's big companies.

- I think I can make a difference to the everyday lives of poor people if I only use materials that are fairly traded.

- If all designers and manufacturers only used fairly traded materials, the world would soon become a much fairer place.

For more information visit:
www.sda-uk.org/sa2.html

Future generations and sustainable design

Are we using resources so fast that there'll be nothing left for the future?

We have only one planet – but in the UK we live as though we had three.

This is because in doing just whatever we want without thinking – using cars, having overseas holidays, keeping our badly insulated building warm with central heating, eating food from far way and out of season – we are using up the resources that belong to future generations.

Fact

One flight to Athens emits 2336 kg of CO2 per passenger. To offset this, a passenger would have to go without heating, cooking, lighting and mechanised transport for two years and nine months. (*The Independent* 28.05.05)

Activity –
Stealing from the future

1. Ask for four volunteers (called A, B, C and D in these instructions). Ask them to stand next to each other, facing the 'audience'.

2. Tell the audience that A represents a parent and that B is his daughter, C is B's son and D is C's daughter. Thus we have four generations. Suggest that A is 35, B is 15 and that C and D have not yet been born – they are the future generations.

3. Give each of them a £10 note or token. Explain that the money represents not cash, but the earth's natural resources – fresh water, timber, oil and so on. Point out that in the interests of fairness everything has been divided evenly – children will naturally see that this is the right thing to do.

4. Interview A. Ask where he would like to go for a holiday of a lifetime – maybe some remote and exotic destination in the tropics. Keep this and all subsequent discussions light so that everyone can have a laugh. Say that this will use quite a lot of oil and cause significant carbon emissions etc., and take the £10 notes from A and B, saying that they have used up their allowance of natural resources.

5. If there is any comment from C or D shut them up, saying that they have not been born yet.

6. Now ask A and B what they would like to do this coming year. Another holiday perhaps? Or maybe a nice new car? Encourage them to aim for something really nice. This has to be paid for by taking the £10 from C, as A and B have already spent their inheritance. Again if C protests point out that he hasn't been born so he cannot say anything.

7. Then do it again – maybe this time buying a new house. Take the £10 from D to pay for it.

8. Now explain that we are sixty years later. A is dead and buried. B has lost her marbles and is in a home. By now C is 30 and D is 5. Ask C what he wants do for a holiday. Almost certainly he will want to take his child somewhere nice – but there are no resources left. If he wants to have a local holiday, point out that due to climate change, pollution etc. this is hardly an attractive proposition. Explain that there are no forests left, nor hardly any natural spaces. There is nowhere for them to go. It is a bleak prospect.

9. Then ask C and D how they feel. Usually they will feel pretty bitter that previous generations have lived so thoughtlessly. Ask A and B how they felt. Usually they will say that they got on with life and enjoyed it. Unpack the experiences as appropriate.

You may wish to say that living as though we have three planets is 'borrowing from the future'. But 'borrowing' implies that we can repay it. Surely it is more accurate to say that we are 'stealing from the future'?

Suitable for all D&T areas

Sustainable schools doorways

8

For more information visit:
www.stepin.org
www.informationinspiration.org.uk

CHOICES

SOCIAL, ECONOMIC AND
ENVIRONMENTAL CHOICES

Becoming an informed decision-maker

Is there a right answer?

As designers and makers we should consider the social, economic and environmental implications of our decisions. They are usually interlinked and don't easily fit into one separate category.

For example, all making involves materials, which take varying amounts of energy to produce and transport. Any use of energy (usually from fossil fuel sources) will cause pollution in a variety of ways and places, and increase climate change. The pollution damages the natural environment and people's health and this leads to economic costs. Climate change is already having a social effect (the WHO calculated that it had led to 150,000 deaths just in the year 2000), is already having economic costs and is also the most serious threat to habitats, biodiversity and landscapes. Additionally, the production of raw materials and products is frequently dependent on low wages and bad working conditions which damage people's health. Recycling is usually seen as having environmental benefits. But it has economic costs, uses energy, often causes air or water pollution and is frequently carried out in places without effective health and safety regulations, where it can have serious effects on the health of workers and others, and damage the local environment.

(www.lboro.ac.uk)

The natural world of plants and animals is absolutely vital for our survival. Biodiversity provides for our needs and cleans up our wastes. Anything which threatens biodiversity has social and economic impacts on our lives as well as financial costs.

Every decision is likely to involve a moral choice as well. There are no right answers, though there are answers that point in the direction of a more sustainable future. The following pages encourage students to become informed decision-makers.

(www.sda-uk.org)

Social responsibility means...

...ensuring that our own and other people's quality of life and human rights are not compromised to fulfil our expectations and demands

If your students are to be well-informed, socially responsible consumers and designers, they should ask the following questions about all products:

- Does the product improve the quality of life for its users?

- Is this product appropriate for the society and culture in which it will be used?

- Does the product encourage the maintenance of traditional knowledge and skills, or could traditional knowledge and skills be lost over time as a result (e.g. home cooking)?

- Does the making of the product (e.g. material or energy used) have a positive or negative impact on the quality of life for some people, including those living elsewhere in the world, sometimes in poverty?

- Does the product help to maintain valuable social or cultural traditions, e.g. the food we eat, clothes we wear, our music, leisure activities?

- Does the product encourage us to be sociable, to enjoy the company of others, when we want to?

- Does the product meet the needs of people today without limiting the ability of future generations to meet their needs satisfactorily?

- Does the making of the product infringe any basic human rights, e.g. fair pay, decent working conditions?

CHOICES

(www.sda-uk.org)

Economic responsibility means...

...considering economic implications of our actions, including ensuring that there is an economic benefit both to the region from which the product came and to the region in which it is marketed

Economically responsible consumers and designers should ask the following questions about all products:

- How will the product impact on employment opportunities? Will there be more or fewer jobs as a result?

- What types of jobs will be created by the product? Will they create or maintain skills?

- Is the production process economically fair to everyone involved in it – whether sourcing materials, transporting, making, using or disposing? Does everyone get a fair deal?

- Where is the employment impact? Does the process encourage local production and employment? Can it help alleviate poverty by fair trade jobs?

- Does the process minimise impacts through energy use and material choice, and therefore cut out unnecessary expenditure? Good design 'does more with less'.

- Can the product be sold without subsidy from elsewhere? Will people want to, and be able to afford to, buy it?

- Who gets the profit? Is anyone exploited?

- How can the process be financed? Can eco-friendly finance be used?

Environmental responsibility means...

...ensuring that our actions and lifestyles don't cause the planet's resources to be used at unsustainable rates

If your students are to be well-informed, environmentally responsible consumers and designers, they should ask the following questions about all products.

When sourcing materials, can environmental impacts be reduced to a minimum by considering:
- where they come from
- whether they are being used at a sustainable rate (can they be replaced as fast as they are extracted?)
- whether local air or water pollution is caused through mining processes or the use of pesticides and fertilisers

- whether any local habitats are damaged in a way they can't recover from quickly (how much overburden has been moved?)
- how much energy has been used in extraction
- how much water has been used
- what visual impact there has been?

When manufacturing products, can environmental impacts be reduced to a minimum by considering, for example:
- energy use
- use of waste products
- pollution
- toxicity
- durability
- disassembly?

In the distribution and sale of products, can environmental impacts be minimised when considering, for example:
- packaging
- storage
- transport
- points of sale?

In the product's use, can environmental impacts be reduced to a minimum through, for example:
- designing for repair
- durability
- low energy use?

When disposing of the product at the end of its life, can environmental impacts be reduced to a minimum by considering, for example:
- design for reuse
- efficient recycling
- toxicity?

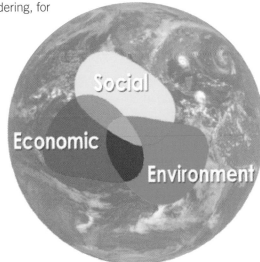

(www.sda-uk.org)

An example – mobile phones

Consumption and design choices in the UK have a big impact on poverty and the lives of communities around the world

We live in an interdependent world where consumer choices in one country have social, economic and environmental impacts on the lives of people many miles away. Some of these connections need unravelling – what does your mobile phone have to do with the lives of people and animals in Africa?

The diagram shows how demand for a material which is used largely in developed countries can lead to displacement of local people and increased conflict in developing countries.

This is an activity to show how social, economic and environmental sustainability issues are often interlinked, and that decisions about designing and making involve making moral choices.

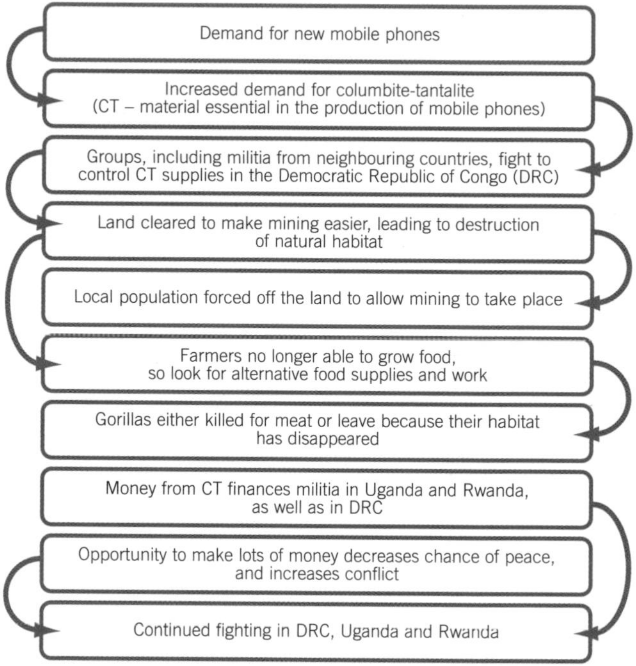

Demand for new mobile phones

Increased demand for columbite-tantalite
(CT – material essential in the production of mobile phones)

Groups, including militia from neighbouring countries, fight to control CT supplies in the Democratic Republic of Congo (DRC)

Land cleared to make mining easier, leading to destruction of natural habitat

Local population forced off the land to allow mining to take place

Farmers no longer able to grow food, so look for alternative food supplies and work

Gorillas either killed for meat or leave because their habitat has disappeared

Money from CT finances militia in Uganda and Rwanda, as well as in DRC

Opportunity to make lots of money decreases chance of peace, and increases conflict

Continued fighting in DRC, Uganda and Rwanda

CHOICES

Activity

- Ask pupils to complete: 'I think mobile phones are good/bad because...'
- Share the facts about CT and the DRC. Pupils could be asked to collect and read this information as a homework exercise. (see overleaf)
- Divide the class into six groups, and give each group a different information card.
- Each group will discuss the information on their card and decide whether CT has a positive or negative impact on the lives of the people. Pupils should be encouraged to think about 'degrees' of impact - completely negative, mostly negative, neutral, mostly positive, completely positive.
- Each group in turn will read their card and say which degree of impact they have chosen, with justification. The results should be recorded to give an overall view.
- Ask for comments on the overall results - do pupils agree with the placements, or should any be changed?
- Ask pupils to go back into their groups and discuss how - if at all - their views on mobile phones have changed.
- Encourage pupils to think of actions they could take to address some of the issues raised as designers, e.g. recycling, reusing, reducing and refusing. Follow up activities could look at these in more depth.
- For a short version of this activity, look at the diagram and discuss the social, economic and environmental impacts of each box, and how this influences the choice of material for a product. Emphasise that it is the attempt to control access to resources, especially CT, that is the cause of continuing conflict.

Suitable for all D&T areas

Sustainable schools doorways

For more information visit:

www.stepin.org

www.informationinspiration.org.uk

CHOICES

Some facts about columbite-tantalite and the DRC

Columbite-tantalite is needed to produce a super heat conductive material which is used to make the modern hi-tech capacitors for mobile phones, computers, nuclear reactors and playstations. There are now more than 2 billion mobile phones connected in the world. The Democratic Republic of the Congo (DRC) in central Africa has a lot of natural resources, including rubber, diamonds and 80% of the world's known reserves of columbite-tantalite. Columbite-tantalite is now a valuable, highly sought after resource. The DRC has been involved in a civil war since the 1960s. Millions of people have been killed, tortured and have had to leave their homes and become refugees. The north-eastern area of the DRC where columbite-tantalite is mined includes national parks which are the natural home of lowland gorillas, elephants and okapi.

This area is a traditional farming area. Militia (soldiers and guerrillas) from neighbouring countries such as Rwanda and Uganda have taken control over much of the mining area. They have made a lot of money from selling columbite-tantalite on the global market to satisfy the demand for hi-tech goods. The average monthly wage in the DRC is $10/month. People's life expectancy is 43 years and falling.

Information for cards

DRC Government

Joseph Kabila is the president of the DRC. He took over when his father, Laurent, was killed by opponents in 2001. Joseph did not want to be president, but he was forced to take over. The government is very weak, and has little power. Joseph had to invite some of the warlords into the government and give them some power. Some of the warlords have their own armies. Joseph does not have an army, and is very isolated.

Militia

There are groups of militia from Uganda and Rwanda who control the mining areas in DRC. Members of the militia are paid very well – up to $60/day. The militia are very powerful, and control the government.

Farmers

The farmers' land has been taken over by the militia, and destroyed by mining. The farmers have lost their traditional livelihoods. Food is not produced on the land any more, and people have to look for other sources of food. Some of the farmers have become miners. Others have been killed by the militia or forced to fight.

Women

Women in the north-eastern area of the DRC can find work in the mining process. One job is carrying heavy loads for the miners. Others are forced to work as prostitutes for the miners who have left their families behind. In the civil war, many women have been raped.

Miners

The columbite-tantalite is dug by hand by groups of miners. It is a dirty and difficult job. Miners can earn high wages – up to $200/month, but many earn far less than this. Often miners will sell the ore, but then the money is stolen by militia. Some of the miners are children, or farmers, and some are prisoners of the militia. Miners do what they need to do to survive. Sometimes they eat meat from gorillas or elephants.

Children

Some children have left school to become miners, hoping to earn money. Sometimes they are captured by the militia and forced to work or fight. Some have also been forced to become sex workers. Children have been killed and injured in the fighting. Schools have closed down as a result of the war.

Suitable for all D&T areas

Sustainable schools doorways

For more information visit:
www.stepin.org
www.informationinspiration.org.uk

ACTION

TAKING PRACTICAL ACTION

Taking practical action in your department

Sustainable design and technology in schools:

- Students are encouraged to **RETHINK** their current way of life, the way we use materials and energy as consumers and designers, and to question whether we can continue to live the way we do now

- Departments **RETHINK** the way they are organised and the way students are taught in order to reflect sustainability principles

- Departments **RETHINK** the design briefs they give students, questioning whether or not the products should be made at all

- Departments try to **REDUCE** their school's environmental impact by setting design briefs that consider the school's energy use, food policy, transport systems, materials procurement

- Students are encouraged to design and make so they **REDUCE** the materials and energy impact of their decisions

- Students are encouraged to **REUSE** materials or products either by dual or multi-purpose design or by reusing them for a second product

- Students are encouraged to design products that can be REPAIRED and to **REPAIR** existing products rather than buying or making new ones

- Students are encouraged to **RECYCLE** materials where it is more appropriate than to use new materials

- Students are encouraged to **REFUSE** to use certain materials in their designs

- Students are encouraged to **REFUSE** to buy or use certain products if they are not needed

- Students are encouraged to evaluate their work at the end of every project and to **REDESIGN** in a more sustainable way.

Ideas

- The eco-bin. Have a set of eco-bins in which all reusable materials from any source are kept, e.g. wood, plastic, textiles. ALL students must look to see if they can reuse any materials from the eco-bins before they look for new materials.

- Waste not... Build compulsory disassembly into projects. Then, if students do not want to take a product home when it's completed, it can be disassembled and put into eco-bins.

- Project folders. Make it compulsory for students to design and make their own project folders from reused or recycled materials only.

- Design briefs. Set design briefs that encourage students to reduce environmental impacts in their schools, e.g. designing and making bicycle carriers.

- Eco-design tools. Ask students to evaluate the sustainability of their projects with a view to improving their sustainability in future work.

- Re-evaluate. Use a design abacus to complete a departmental sustainability audit.

Taking practical action in food areas

Sustainable food technology is a food area where:

- We **RETHINK** schemes of work so that students have the opportunity to use creative designing to rethink the use of healthy foods such as broccoli

- We **RETHINK** schemes of work so that sustainable design is an integral part of the way teachers teach and students think

- We **RETHINK** with students the average high-animal-product diet, discussing the big impact in land use, energy and methane emissions (adding to climate change)

- We **REFUSE** to use genetically modified ingredients and actively encourage the use of organic ingredients

- We **REFUSE** to use food produced using child labour and actively encourage the use of fair-trade ingredients

- We **REFUSE** to use out of season ingredients that have been air-freighted across the world using up lots of 'food miles', and actively encourage the use of local, in-season ingredients

- We **REDUCE** food waste by using recipes with fewer than five ingredients

- We **REDUCE** food waste by incorporating knowledge of portion sizes, e.g. pasta and rice, into lesson plans

- We **REDUCE** the energy used during practical activities by encouraging one-pan cooking, sharing ovens and fewer uses of electrical equipment such as a processor

- We **REDUCE** the energy used by including raw food recipes in schemes of work

- We **REDUCE** the effect on students' health of the food products they make by using balanced recipes, low in fat, sugar and salt

- We **REDUCE** the use of processed ingredients and raise awareness of their large impact

- We **REUSE** leftover ingredients in future practical activities and include using leftover foods in schemes of work

- We **REPAIR** equipment and cookers rather than buying new ones

- We **RECYCLE** tins, plastic bottles and glass as well as paper and card.

Ideas

- Waste disposal. Have four different bins for recycling tins, plastics, glass, and paper and card.

- Healthy eating. Use schemes of work that consistently promote the Balance of Good Health through both key stages where using fruit and vegetables (sometimes in their raw state) are key to practicals every year.

- How 'safe' is your food? Incorporate issues discussed during citizenship lessons such as fair-trade products and child labour into evaluations of practical activities.

Sustainable Schools

England

The Sustainable Schools Framework highlights the important role schools can play in securing a sustainable future. It identifies three areas in which a school can show its commitment to sustainable development – through its curriculum, its campus and its links with the community.

This resource reflects the aims of that document and the activities link to the eight doorways it identifies. The doorways are different ways of approaching the task of building a school that exemplifies a culture of sustainability.

Where relevant, each activity identifies numerically which doorway it supports. They are:

[1] Food and drink

[2] Energy and water

[3] Travel and traffic

[4] Purchasing and waste

[5] Buildings and grounds

[6] Inclusion and participation

[7] Local well-being

[8] Global dimension.

For more information on the eight gateways go to; http://www.se-ed.co.uk/ sustainable-schools/ resources/Brief and visit the Sustainable Schools Alliance www.sustainable-schools-alliance.org.uk

Wales

Wales is one of very few countries in the world with a commitment to Sustainable Development built into the constitution.

The Education for Sustainable Development and Global Citizenship Action Plan, which was published in September 2006,

is a strategic approach, rather than guidance for schools. Such guidance will be one of the next steps.

The Action Plan promotes the idea of working through award schemes such as Eco-schools, but also Ysgolion Gwyrdd in Gwynedd and the Pembrokeshire Sustainable Schools Scheme.

1. Food & drink

2. Energy & water

3. Travel & traffic

4. Purchasing & waste

5. Buildings & grounds

6. Inclusion & participation

7. Local well-being

8. Global dimension

Taking practical action on material choices

Choosing materials for a product (or building, or anything else you make) is ALWAYS a matter of judgement. When you think about materials you can consider sustainability issues such as scarcity, use of energy, toxicity, how much water is used, and whether or not it is available locally. What is the impact on biodiversity in extracting or growing the raw material, in processing it, using it in the manufacture of products? What happens to materials at the end of the product's life?

Key issues when choosing materials:

- Properties – working properties, chemical properties, aesthetics, fitness for purpose etc. – all the things that students think about anyway.

- Scarcity and renewability of sources. The carbon footprint of a particular material

- Is it needed? Can it be ethically sourced?

- How far it has travelled? – local is better

- The embodied energy and toxicity over the whole life cycle (this will include impact on biodiversity)

- Is it recycled? Can it be recycled after use?

- Cost.

1. RETHINK materials: we tend to think that 'natural' is better than 'synthetic'. It is certainly better to choose renewable materials than finite ones. Natural does not always mean 'no impact' (see opposite). Sometimes a synthetic material is simply the best – such as using polymer-based damp-proofing in buildings.

It's natural – no impact?

Cotton needs a lot of water to grow, and most cotton grows in places that are short of water.

Paper bags use up trees and are heavier than plastic bags to transport.

Leather tanning is very polluting.

Biodegradable packaging materials are made from plants, so:

- They take land to grow
- They will degrade into something eventually and give off CO2 or methane
- They often require a lot of energy to process them.

So are oil-based materials bettcr?

- Oil and gas are finite
- Plastic production is also polluting
- Many plastic products either cannot be or are not recycled.

2. REFUSE materials: are they toxic in themselves – for example, asbestos, mercury?

Are people exploited in their production? (See www.fairtrade.org.uk for information about goods that are ethically sourced.)

Can you refuse unnecessary packaging?

3. REDUCE materials: think about the embodied energy and the toxic impact of the product. How far have the different materials travelled? More travel means more energy and more toxic emissions. How much energy has gone into making the materials? And what toxic emissions are there? This includes sourcing original materials, processing and manufacture.

(www.sda-uk.org)

What happens at the end of life? Can more be done with less material? This is the ultimate win-win-win: lower cost, less energy, fewer toxic emissions, altogether less impact.

4. RECYCLE materials: recycling matcrials is usually better than not recycling, but sometimes it uses more energy to recycle than to produce virgin materials. Think about recyclability. (Just because a product has a recycling logo it does not follow that it can be recycled.)

ACTION

Material choices in your school rooms

Do some materials have more impact than others?

Facts

We're using more and more wood-based products every year.

Hardwoods can be very sustainable if from local well managed source where the forest is replanted, but very damaging if tropical hardwood (e.g. mahogany)

(www.cat.org.uk)

Softwood – is it from FSC accredited timber?

Plywood – is often made from tropical hardwoods, but you can get fairly local birch-faced plywood

MDF – dust and adhesives used are unhealthy

Alternative materials for window frames:

Metal – inefficient (conducts heat) but long lasting

Plastic (PVC) – polluting from processing, through use, to disposal

Wood – good insulator, long life with maintenance, particularly if hardwood

Principles of good wood choice

- Repair, restore or adapt something you already have

- Buy second-hand, recycled, reclaimed or waste timber

- Buy locally produced timber products that are Forest Stewardship Council (FSC) certified

- Buy FSC certified products from further afield. (Wasteonline)

Forestry Stewardship Council

If you see this logo on timber, it means the wood has come from well-managed forests and it is not contributing to our loss of global forests.

Inspirational product

Treske make furniture from English hardwood sourced from sustainable forests.

Activity

Explore materials in the room you are in

· What materials have been used for the tables, chairs and other furniture? Have they been built to last?

Discuss the most important points to consider when you are choosing whether or not to use wood. Should you use it at all?

Make me a renewable source

Plant a willow tree in Year 7 and you'll be able to use it in later years and keep cutting branches every 1-3 years.

Make me less damaging

Split the students into groups. Tell them to go and stand by an example of materials in use in a product or piece of furniture or the structure of the room itself and get them and the rest of the group to work out:

· Why that material has been used
· Where it comes from
· What its impact is
· Is it durable?
· Was it the best material to use for that job?
· What alternative materials could have been used?

Then make a plan for less damaging materials – get the students to work in pairs and pull it all together in a plenary session.

For more information visit:

www.fsc.org/en/

Sustainable Lifestyles p.110 (information about sustainability and different wood), available from education@practicalaction.org.uk

www.treske.co.uk

www.wasteonline.org.uk

Taking practical action in energy choices

The big issue around energy is that some countries use *far too much*. Secondly we are madly careless in the use of fossil fuels. Burning them contributes to climate change.

Facts

- More than 50% of the world's energy is used by 15% of the world's population. (World Bank)
- Cycling rather than driving 3 miles saves 2 kg of carbon.
- Catching Eurostar to Paris instead of flying would release 40 times fewer global warming pollutants.
- Turning down your heating by 1°C saves around 250 kg of CO_2 over an average winter. (*I Count: Your step-by-step guide to climate bliss.* Penguin Books)
- Every cup of liquid boiled is 25 more cups of carbon. (www. chooseclimate.org)

A supply of energy is critical to help people escape poverty. It cooks the food we eat. It lights homes so that children can study in the evening. It keeps vaccines cool. It powers businesses.

- Two billion people (40% of the world's population) have no modern energy services.
- In sub-Saharan Africa, 80% of people do not have access to electricity. Those without power usually live in remote rural or poor urban areas. (www. practicalaction.org.uk)

In rethinking the way we use energy we need innovation, low-carbon technologies and less energy-intensive lifestyles. This is the challenge for designers and consumers. Some of the questions we should ask are:

- How can we reduce the energy we use?
- Walk or cycle or bus instead of car? Train instead of plane?
- Turn down the heating? Get better home insulation?
- When we buy an electrical product do we consider how much energy it uses day to day?
- Do we actually need that new item?
- Do we really need to make that trip?
- Can we make more use of renewable sources?
- Can we sign up for 'green electricity' at home?

ACTION

Product story

Currently in Sri Lanka, families may have to travel long distances and wait long times for their batteries to be recharged at commercial centres. Small-scale windpower generators have the potential for either community or private use. Around 300,000 vehicle batteries are currently in household use, so the demand is vast.

The average electricity consumption per household in the country is approximately 68 kWh per month. Small wind turbine systems, with a capacity ranging from 50 W to 10 kW and rotor diameter ranging from about 0.5 m to 7 m, are primarily used in battery charging. These applications include energy supply for houses (lighting, TV, refrigerator), hospitals, farms and communication.

Security

We assume that gas and electricity must always be available 24/7. This argument is used to justify the building of nuclear power stations. Discuss in groups: Is this what we really want? Can we achieve energy security in other ways? Can we make more use of renewable energies?

For more information visit:

www.practicalaction.org/practicalanswers (renewable energy projects)

www.practicalaction.org/practicalanswers (technical information)

www.cat.org.uk

www.energysavingtrust.org.uk/

Energy and trees

Can planting trees save the planet?

Facts

Planes are powered by fossil fuel oil. When you take a flight the oil is burned and this gives off CO2 emissions, which contribute hugely to global warming. However, you can now buy 'carbon offsets'. This means that someone else plants trees to absorb the CO2 given off by your energy use.

The challenge

What message does this give people? Is it, 'Now I can fly as much as I like!'? But can we plant our way out of trouble? If we are using more than the planet can provide already, where do they put the trees? We haven't got those two extra planets.

What does it cost to plant the trees? It is about £13.50 for a return flight to the USA (that pays to plant the trees – but they take 25 years to absorb the CO2). 'If we wanted enough trees to cope with all our home-grown carbon pollution we would need to plant a new area of tropical forest more than 1.5 times the size of the entire UK. It won't work.' (*I Count: Your step-by-step guide to climate bliss.* Penguin) How can we put a price on climate change?

So we should plant trees, but let's not kid ourselves that it will do much to save the planet …

Stop Climate Injustice

Climate change is killing the developing world
www.practicalaction.org/climatechange

PRACTICAL ACTION

Product story

At the Centre for Alternative Technology in Machynlleth in Wales we use lots of timber in our buildings. But we use all sorts of other materials as well. Some visitors say 'You shouldn't be using all that wood!' and others say 'Why isn't it all wood?' So what is the story of the tree and timber?

A tree absorbs CO2 as it grows and stores the carbon as carbohydrates. When it reaches maturity it stops absorbing extra carbon. Eventually, if not cut down, it will die and gradually give off CO2 as it decays, but only what was absorbed recently – this is very different from burning fossil fuels. Alternatively, wood can be used for products such as furniture or buildings which lock up the carbon during their lifetime.

What is the most efficient way to manage woodland? We could grow trees to maturity, cut them down, use them and replant. That would work well in terms of them absorbing CO2 from the atmosphere. But then we'd never have any of those ancient oaks and beeches. Does that matter?

(www.cat.org.uk)

(www.cat.org.uk)

Make me aware

Discuss the issues, then ask students to design a poster to raise awareness about how planting trees does not actually do much to mitigate the effects of flying. Alternatively, put together a short dramatic sketch that can be performed at a school assembly.

Graphics

Sustainable schools doorways

 2 . 8

For thinking behind carbon offsets, see:
www.carbontrust.co.uk/carbon/briefing/offsets.htm and www.carbonfootprint.com/carbon_offset.html.

For a critique of carbon offsetting, see: www.risingtide.org.uk/.

THE SIX Rs

RE... When is it OK to use recycled materials?

REDUCE How can we use less stuff?

REUSE Can we use things again?

How can we design products for repair?

...an we ...ferently?

REUSE

what should I do?

RETHINK

THE SIX Rs
Activities for students

The six Rs – what are they?

Activity

Give students jumbled sets of R words and definitions. Ask them to link each word to the definition they think fits it best. Discuss and give suggested answers. Then ask students to look at the images and suggest which R word (or words) would best fit each image.

RETHINK

Take an existing product that's become waste, and use the material or parts for another purpose, without processing it.

REUSE

Don't use a material or buy a product if you think you don't need it or if it's unsustainable.

RECYCLE

Minimise the amount of material and energy you use.

REPAIR

Ask whether we can sustain our current way of life and the way we design and make.

REDUCE

When a product breaks down or doesn't function properly, try to fix it.

REFUSE

Take an existing product that has become waste and reprocess the material to use in a new product.

Replacing parts in a computer.

Sharing lifts to school with friends.

A dress made only from natural materials

Packaging of a bottle on a supermarket shelf.

Darning socks

A biodegradable roadside memorial

A bar stool made mainly from old car parts

An Apple iPhone

This lampshade was made from old photographic slides.

A chair made from reused carpet rolls and magazines

Nike used to have 18 different shoe boxes. Now they have one with no glues or staples.

The body of this guitar was made from plastic sheets from recycled yoghurt pots.

Suitable for all D&T areas

Sustainable schools doorways

2   4

The six Rs spinner

Redesign me

- Make the 6Rs spinner, using a pencil for its axis - describe its purpose.

- Organise students into groups. Give each group an example of a product that is no longer working or needed. Try to disassemble the product carefully. If this is not possible, discuss the implications.

- Each member of the group, in turn, spins the 6Rs spinner. Whichever 'R' the spinner lands on, the group should brainstorm the issues.

- Use the key questions grid to help set the scene.

- Sketch ideas for a redesign of the product.

- Using the title 'Sustainable Design is Great Design', share your ideas for the product's redesign with other groups.

- Display your work in a prominent place for the whole school to see.

Reduce

Which parts are not needed?

Do we need as much material?

Can we simplify the product?

....

....

....

....

Reuse

Which parts can I use again?

Has it another valuable use without processing it?

....

....

....

....

Repair

Which parts can be replaced?

Which parts are going to fail?

How easy is it to replace parts?

....

....

....

....

Recycle

How easy is to take apart?

How can the parts be used again?

How much energy to reprocess parts?

....

....

....

....

Refuse

Is it really necessary?

Is it going to last?

Is it fair trade?

....

....

....

....

Rethink

How can it do the job better?

Is it energy efficient?

Has it been designed for disassembly?

....

....

....

....

Suitable for all D&T areas

Sustainable schools doorways

RETHINK
our current lifestyles and the way
we design and make

Needs and wants

As designers, do we have a responsibility to design and make only for what people need or for what they want? What *do* we need beyond the basics?

'Once you have enough food, shelter and the basic means of survival, additional income does not seem to make people any happier.' (New Economics Foundation)

'The world has enough for everyone's need, but not for everyone's greed.' (Mahatma Gandhi)

Activity: All you need is...

- Ask your class what we need for basic survival (food, water, shelter).

- Put them in groups and ask them to discuss what we need for a fulfilled life. Tell them to imagine they have the food, water and shelter but no one and nothing else. They need to decide what they need to make life worth living.

- Give them lists of things they might want or need or they could just come up with their own ideas.

- Ask them to agree on the three needs they think are the most important (you might say five or get them to put them all in order).

- Each group reports back and class discusses which are the most important needs in our society.

- Discuss the role of music, art and beauty. Do we need beautiful objects, buildings etc? What effect do these things have on us?

- Ask them whether their top needs are things that have a big impact on the planet and people. Are they unsustainable because of the energy used or pollution caused? Can we provide them for everyone on the planet?

- What is the difference between needs and wants?

- What approach to needs should we take when we are designing? Should we try to meet all the different needs? Should we think about what people want? What about designing beautiful things to make people feel good?

Suitable for all D&T areas

Sustainable schools doorways

The 'Make Me' Wheel

How can we encourage students to include sustainability issues into all their design briefs?

Facts

- About 20 tonnes of waste are produced for every one tonne of product that reaches the consumer.

- If every European household replaced three incandescent bulbs with low-energy compact fluorescents then the energy saved would allow us to close ten 600 MW power stations!

RETHINK

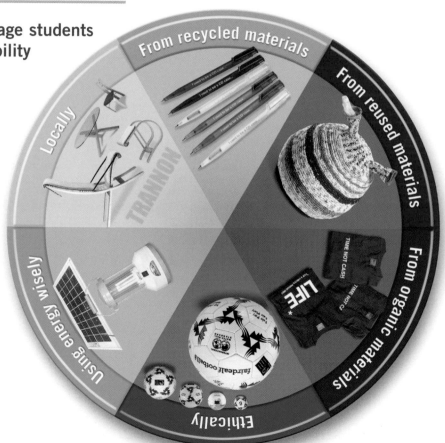

Activities

- At the start, remind students that their product must have a sustainable design element to it.

- Students have to design and make a cushion in their textile technology class (see below for other focus area suggestions). They must incorporate a sustainability element.

- Spin the MAKE ME wheel to decide which element of sustainability you will look at first, e.g. with reused materials.

- Ask students to mind-map suggestions about how they might include 'reused materials' into their specification (e.g. discarded buttons, offcuts, old clothes).

- Repeat with other MAKE ME criteria to give students more ideas.

- Ask each student either to spin the wheel or to decide on her/his sustainability criterion for the cushion. Their design must now include that criterion. Use the ideas generated by the class mind-mapping exercise.

Ideas for other focus areas

Graphics: A desk calendar

Food: A pasta dish

Product design: A piece of furniture

Systems and control: Any electronic product

Suitable for all D&T areas

Sustainable schools doorways

 2 4

Personal audit line-up

Are we aware of the sustainability consequences of our buying and designing decisions?

The purpose of the line-up activity is to get students to think about their current behaviour and to RETHINK whether there are ways in which they could change to help make the world a more sustainable place.

Ideas for other focus areas

Textiles: the last article of clothing you bought

Graphics: the last DVD bought

Product design/Systems and control: the last product bought

Activity: Line-ups

- Ask students to bring in to your lesson their favourite snack or drink (see opposite for ideas appropriate to other focus areas).

- Ask all the students to think about the materials needed to make the product. When they bought it did they think about any of the following material choices:
  - Were workers involved in production fairly paid?
  - Were any pesticides or fertilisers used?
  - How far had ingredients travelled to reach your shop?
  - How much processing was involved (and so energy use)?
  - Are any of the ingredients in short supply?

- Choose 6-8 students and ask them to stand from left to right of classroom according to how much or how little they thought about those issues before choosing the product.

- Repeat using end of life ideas
  - Can the packaging be reused for anything?
  - Can the packaging be recycled?
  - Will the product go into landfill and if so, is it biodegradable?

- Now ask students to consider their personal choices and assess whether the product is sustainable. Ask 6-8 students to stand on a sustainability continuum and justify how good or bad their product is.

- Ask students to consider whether they could buy differently to make a more positive environmental impact.

Suitable for all D&T areas

Sustainable schools doorways

 2 4

For more information visit:

www.sda-uk.org/sa3.html
(explains other ways of using line-ups)

www.newint.org/issues/
(particularly Nov 2006)

www.adbusters.org/home/

Seasonal foods

Is it OK to use any ingredients, wherever they've come from?

Many of us living in the UK have grown to expect the foods we like to be available all year round. This has enormous impact on the environment and on people involved in food production.

Asparagus is only in season in the UK for two months of the year: May and June. However, it is available in supermarkets all year round. It comes from Italy or Spain for a few months. For over six months of the year it is flown in from Peru.

Since the 1950s there's been a massive decrease in orchards in the UK. Instead of being available to buy from the UK, apples are being transported from New Zealand, South Africa, etc. Visit a supermarket to find out the countries fruit is imported from.

Apples transported from South Africa have travelled over 5,000 miles.

Food miles are a way of attempting to measure how far food has travelled before it reaches the consumer. It is a good way of looking at the environmental impact of foods and their ingredients.

What can we do?

Buy local! That's the key. This means supporting local growers. It's much better for the environment if you grow and/or buy organic.

Activities

Select a range of foods (or labels) from overseas and ask students to write down their country of origin. Think about the distance travelled, then think about how that distance was covered. Was it by plane? Boat? Truck?

Look at examples of how many miles food has travelled. This will give students a measurement of the pollution that is caused by the different methods of transporting that food to the UK.

Make me locally

Design and make a meal using seasonal and local ingredients.

Introduce the concepts of seasonal foods and food miles by having an Apple Day. Ask each student to bring in an apple. Make a distance line from those picked in the garden to those that have come the furthest, e.g. New Zealand or South Africa. Record on a map or in graph form showing food miles. Discuss.

Have a tasting session of different apples. Include a fun competition of who can produce the longest piece of peel. Extend this lesson with focused tasks on apples. Complete the same project with tomatoes.

Get students to produce monthly posters of seasonal foods with recipes. Use celebrity chefs such as Hugh Fearnley-Whittingstall or Nigel Slater.

Food technology

Sustainable schools doorways

Food miles calculator:
www.organiclinker.com/food-miles.ctm

For further ideas visit:
www.stepin.org/index.php?id=fft_brief
www.organicfood.co.uk
www.soilassociation.co.uk
www.eattheseasons.co.uk/

Energy sources

Do we always need to use electricity?

Every day we carry out many of our tasks using electrically powered products. We give very little thought to the energy source powering the product or whether we could carry out the same task without it. For example, when we need to do some arithmetic we automatically reach for a calculator.

Inspirational product

The One Laptop Per Child (OLPC) wind-up laptop computer eliminates the need for batteries by relying on the user to provide the energy to run it.

Activity

Ask yourself the following 'rethink' questions.

- Do I need a calculator? Could the arithmetic be done without it?
- How is it powered? Could it be powered differently?
- Is it solar powered? If it is battery powered, how long before replacement?

You could adapt these questions for another product, such as a torch or radio.

Make me simple

- Make a list of electrical or electronic products that you use regularly. Using the calculator example, adapt the 'rethink' questions; think of some additional ones.

When you next buy an electronic product use your answers to help you choose a more sustainable design.

- Design and make a system or product that converts one source of energy to another. Visit the CAT and TEP websites for ideas to help. Keep it simple and low cost. Take photographs of your project, as it develops, to produce a wall display.

Sustainable schools doorways

2

For more information visit:

www.informationinspiration.org.uk

www.cat.org.uk (Centre for Alternative Technology)

www.tep.org.uk (Technology Enhancement Project)

www.mutr.co.uk (TEP resources)

Promoting sustainability

How can we encourage sustainable communities?

For a sustainable society to exist, it must be economically viable, as well as environmentally sound and socially just. For a product to succeed in the market, customers must want to buy it, and there is a strong chance that sustainable products might cost more. Local production, organic farming and fair trade all have potential costs, as well as benefits.

So, in order to help promote products and lifestyles that might lead to a more sustainable society, it might be necessary to adapt some of the tools of consumerism.

Inspirational product

It is not only products, but also homes, schools and other buildings where the designer needs to give sustainability sufficient thought. Coventry City Council has a strategy plan for its schools which includes Environment days, a Democracy Project and many other ideas which might be useful to you.

It has also included sustainable design features, such as grey water and a 'sedum roof' in its newly built schools, such as Moseley Primary School. Sedum is a green, grass-type plant, which will provide a habitat for local insects and birds, whilst absorbing rainwater.

Living roof for eco-friendly new school
(Coventry City Council press release)

RETHINK

Activities

- Discuss what makes you want to buy products and services, and list some of the ways that more sustainable approaches could be promoted.

- Consider some of the purchases which you have made recently. Write down the factors that you considered when deciding to buy, and list some of the other factors you could have thought about.

Make me desirable

- Design a point of sale display for fair trade products to go into a school canteen. Consider the possibility of making this a 'flat-pack' product.

- Design publicity material for your school or department that would reflect a greater 'sustainability identity'.

- Design special promotional material, perhaps a board game, for sending to new students explaining how they can fit into and contribute to the school's sustainable community.

- Redesign a facility which is important from a sustainability perspective (e.g. a bicycle shelter) and make a 3-D model showing the improvements

- Make a 3-D model of part of your school which illustrates both the current design and improvements which could be made in order to make it more sustainable (e.g. materials, energy, lighting, heating)

(Coventry City Council Agenda 21 website)

For more information visit:

www.stepin.org

www.informationinspiration.org.uk

Cotton, the most natural thing in the world?

Is use of cotton necessarily sustainable?

When we think about organic production we usually focus on food, but huge amounts of chemicals are used to produce cotton.

Facts

- Cotton is a vital commodity for many developing countries and a vital source of income for many of the world's poorest farmers. However, the conventional cotton industry has a devastating effect on farmers, textile workers and the environment.

- The World Health Organisation estimates that 20,000 people a year die in developing countries from pesticide poisoning, and a further 3 million people suffer chronic health problems. Many of these are cotton farmers: worldwide, while conventional cotton farming uses only 3% of total farmland, it consumes 10% of chemical pesticides, and 22% of all insecticides.

- A 100% cotton T-shirt contains only 73% cotton. The rest is made up of chemicals and resins used to grow and make the T-shirt.

- Cotton is the world's most sprayed crop. It is sprayed 8-10 times a season, taking 17 teaspoons of chemicals to raise the 225 g (9 oz) of cotton needed to make a T-shirt.

- Once the cotton has been grown, toxic chemicals are used in many of the manufacturing stages such as pre-treatment, dyeing and printing.

Inspirational products

Howies design quality products made from certified organic cotton. (www.howies.co.uk)

Activities

- Find out about how and where cotton is grown around the world. Find out why cotton is used as a fibre. What are its advantages and disadvantages?

- Identify some clothes/textiles products in your home that contain cotton.

- Find out the meaning of the word organic and do a Product Pairs exercise (see www.sda-uk.org) with one organic and one non-organic T-shirt. What are the main differences between organic and non-organic T-shirts?

Sustainable schools doorways

Teaching Materials:

Real Price of Cotton by Ken Webster, Norfolk Education & Action for Development 2002

There are four main activities contained in this pack: Cotton Choices, the Real Price of Cotton, Cotton Fields and a Case Study of Organic Cotton. Age/level: GCSE Each activity takes approximately 1 hour.

Available from www.labourbehindthelabel.org or www.nead.org.uk

For more information visit:

www.sda-uk.org (for help on materials)
www.newint.org/easier-english?/Garment/cotton-p.html (information on environmental issues linked to cotton production)
www.stepin.org (case study on organic cotton)
www.peopletree.co.uk (organic cotton and fair-trade products)
www.seasaltshop.co.uk (organic clothing)
www.ecomall.com (environmentally sound textiles companies)

RETHINK

What price beauty?

What's the point of a sustainable world if we can't enjoy ourselves?

How important is our need for beautiful and artistic things? How can we satisfy this need in a low-impact way?

'Children need the arts as much as they need fresh air, otherwise they perish on the inside.' (Philip Pullman)

Inspirational product

Heidi Butler creates witty jewellery from laser-cut pieces of recycled plastic and reclaimed wood.

Make me Beautiful
But Low impact

- For homework ask students to research jewellery made from materials with low environmental impact (e.g. made from reused or easily replaceable materials).

- Identify the materials they have discovered that could be used in your D&T class.

- Design and make a piece of jewellery that you would wear for a special occasion, e.g. a birthday party, a disco.

Activities: Are diamonds a girl's best friend?

- Collect jewellery or catalogues with lots of jewellery made from different materials in them. Ask students to work in small groups and jot down as many different materials as they can that are used to make jewellery. Collect all ideas together. Add any others you can think of.

- Discuss what makes a piece of jewellery valuable. How important is what it is made from? How important is where or who it came from? How important is whether or not it is fashionable?

- Ask if anyone has a favourite piece of jewellery they are wearing or have at home, or something that one of their family thinks is special. Ask them to describe it and to explain why it is valuable.

- Do different societies and different cultures have different views of what is valuable? Look at different websites, images of different cultural jewellery and identify what other materials are used in other cultures. Add to the list.

- Go back into groups and choose three different materials from the list. Using scrap paper, write the name of one material in the middle and mind-map all the impacts that producing the material and making it into jewellery might have. Repeat for the other materials.

- They will have vastly different impacts, from almost no-impact found materials to diamonds and gold where huge amounts of earth are moved to get a very small amount of material, workers are often paid very little and work in dreadful conditions, and ground and water pollution are considerable.

- Discuss whether we can make beautiful jewellery without adverse impacts. How much impact is worth it for the beauty we create?

For more information visit:

www.recycle2shop.com/products1.cfm?CategoryID=26693

www.naturalcollection.com/natural-products/Tagua-Nut-Necklace.asp

www.cobraonline.com/

www.slowdesign.org/pdf/Slow%20design.pdf
(a long but interesting view from Alistair Fuad-Luke, author of *The eco-design handbook*, on rethinking how and why we design)

www.co-design.co.uk/mpress.htm
(a shorter discussion relating to waste products)

Efficient food preparation

Can we reduce the energy we use when cooking at home?

Facts

- Food, drink and catering produces about one tenth of our CO_2 emissions in Britain (2.1 tonnes per year of the 20.7t per household). This includes the large contribution to CO_2 from eating out and take-aways.

- Food energy use from field to plate: 30% of the total is used in the home in the storage, preparation and cooking of food.

- Gas cookers use less fossil fuel than electricity. Much of our electricity is produced by burning gas in power stations where it is burned much less efficiently than in a gas cooker.

Product story

In many situations in developing countries charcoal is the only fuel people have available and they have to cook inside without chimneys. The wood to produce the charcoal is becoming more and more scarce in many places. The charcoal is expensive and leads to many health problems and, as a result, people have developed techniques and new designs of stove to burn the fuel as efficiently as possible. They also put chimneys into their homes where practical to do so.

Inspirational product

The storm kettle is designed to boil water using a small amount of kindling (twigs, dry grass etc.) which is burned in a central chamber.

Activities

Look at the energy rating on the fridge and freezer. If possible use an energy meter to find out how much electricity it uses. Work out how much it will use in a week and how much that will cost. Discuss how this energy could be reduced.

How can you rethink energy use when cooking at home? For example, use a pressure cooker or steamer? Put lids on pots?

Make me more efficient

Barbecues are a popular summer activity. They burn charcoal (wood which has been already 'burned' without oxygen). The charcoal is often imported, frequently from places where its use is causing deforestation, but it could be made of locally grown willow or hazel, both fast-growing species which can be coppiced. This involves cutting the branches off about every three years. New branches grow from the stump so there is no need to plant a new tree.

When it is burned charcoal gives off CO_2 and various pollutants, so people are advised never to burn it indoors.

Most barbecues in Britain are very inefficient, with much of the energy escaping to heat the surrounding air, not the food. Disposable barbecues with the metal tray, produced with a large energy and mineral extraction impact, are thrown away after being used only once.

Can you design a more efficient barbecue?

Sustainable schools doorways

REFUSE

REFUSE
Don't accept a product at all if you don't need it or if it's environmentally or socially unsustainable

Refuse these materials and products!

Should we make this product at all?

Facts

There are some materials you should avoid in all designs because of their toxicity – including CFCs, asbestos, PCBs, carbon tetrachloride, lead chromate, mercury.

The sustainability of some other products is questionable from a social, economic or environmental viewpoint.

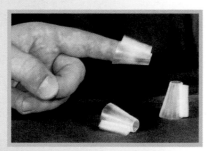

Activities – Room 101

Imagine you are a celebrity invited to appear on the TV show, 'Room 101', where you have the chance to nominate any products you think should be sent to Room 101, which means they will never be seen again.

You are a sustainability expert. You want to get rid of the most unsustainable, pointless products you can think of. However, you will be asked to justify your choices to the presenter. Research some of the products in your chosen focus area, and choose one you want to ban forever. Look at the questions you might be asked by the presenter and get your answers ready. Finally, discuss whether something else could do the same job with less impact.

Room 101 questions

Product design –
An electric toothbrush

- I thought dentists tell us that electric toothbrushes are good for your teeth. Aren't they right?

- What are they made of that we perhaps needn't be using?

- How much energy do they use in an average week? Is it bad?

- What happens to them if they break down? Can we repair them?

- Most of them have replaceable heads. Surely that's a good thing?

- So, if you think electric brushes are so bad, what's the most sustainable way for us to clean our teeth?

Products for other focus areas

Food: A frozen black forest gateau

Textiles: A dyed, non-organic T-shirt made in Indonesia

Graphics: Plastic wrapping, foam trays and promotional material on fruit and vegetables.

Systems and control: Disposable alkaline batteries, Patio heater.

Food packaging, processing and transport

What factors should determine the ingredients we use?

Food is the largest single factor affecting our eco-footprint. Packaging, processing and transport use huge amounts of energy and discarded packaging creates massive waste.

Facts

- In Brazil thousands of children pick oranges to be made into concentrate and processed into juice. They are often exposed to high levels of pesticide and may be paid as little as 13p an hour (www.sustain.co.uk).

- Instant mash is convenient but potatoes have to be washed, peeled, chopped, cooked, freeze-dried and packaged by machines.

- Some cheese-makers now use a genetically modified product instead of rennet but don't have to label the cheese as GM as the cheese itself is not modified.

- Some well-known sea-fish, like cod, are becoming scarce. Farmed fish is becoming more common.

So, why might we REFUSE to use or choose to use some ingredients or products in our food technology?

Activities

- Carry out a Food Product Pairs activity - use fair trade fruit and non-FT fruit, organic and non-organic chocolate, locally grown and imported fruit, free-range and non free-range eggs, over-packaged and non-packaged biscuits. Discuss what influences their original choices. Should we refuse to use any of the products for any reason? Discuss advantages and disadvantages of local, FT, organic, packaging, free-range.

- Investigate the range of FT ingredients there are to use. Why is it important to use these products? Look at the production of orange juice in particular - use 'Taking the Pith' report from www.sustain.co.uk

- Research genetically modified foods, including the number of GM foods in a supermarket. How large is the information telling you that there are GM ingredients in a product? Discuss why GM foods have become increasingly available. Are they necessarily a bad thing?

- Look at the life cycle of a product such as a pizza - how could you make it less processed?

- Investigate the processes involved in fish farming. Is it safe? Investigate and try unusual fish, e.g. char, gurnard.

- Do a product analysis of different kinds of yoghurt such as organic, low fat, bio. Work out which is the most sustainable - including packaging.

- Do a comparison of packaging for biscuits where some have just one layer (e.g. farmhouse), others two or three. Discuss the contrasting demands of hygiene, shelf-life and sustainability. Is all the packaging necessary?

Make me fair

Find examples of products using FT ingredients (e.g. Respect Banana Cake) Could you develop a similar product? (www.stepin.org/index.php?id=ff_home)

Make me with thought

Research products that are available locally and are also organic. Develop a food product that uses only local or organic ingredients. (www.stepin.org/index.php?id=fft_brief)

Food technology

For more information visit:
www.organicfood.co.uk
www.soilassociation.org
www.sustain.co.uk

Ethical electronics

Is being trendy always sustainable?

Advertisers are aware of the potential spending power of most age groups, especially young people and the so-called 'baby-boomers' born in the 1960s. We are encouraged to buy more electronic products and led to believe that a new item works better, or looks better, than a similar purchase made not that long ago.

Consumer electronics has followed the lead from fashion and music, and indeed these technologies have merged with an exponential synergy. The result is must-have products, which satisfy the drives of want and need.

The economic, environmental and ethical consequences are increasingly reported in newspaper headlines, such as:

'Dumped electrical goods: A giant problem'. In the same article, the sub-heading, **'Fashion beats functionality in a throwaway society'**, Martin Hickman, The *Independent*, 27 February 2006, news.independent.co.uk/ environment/article347941.ece

'iPod City', The *Mail on Sunday*, 11 June 2006. The original report is unavailable on-line, but see a summary at:
'Inside Apple's iPod factories' (www.macworld.co.uk/news/index. cfm?RSS&NewsID=14915)

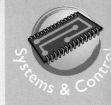

Child labour, collection and recycling, fair trade, human rights, and working conditions are among the ethical issues raised in the manufacture, marketing and disposal of consumer electronics. The major manufacturers have supplier codes of conduct, downloadable from their websites.

Activities

- Brainstorm economic, environmental and ethical issues surrounding consumer electronics. Search the internet to find out more about manufacturers' commitments to them.

- Identify key questions to ask retailers before buying a product. What answers would be acceptable before a purchase is made?

- Produce a poster linking your findings to a product's life cycle.

Sustainable schools doorways

General guidelines are available from:

www.ethicaltrade.org (Ethical Trading Initiative)

www.ilo.org/public/english/standards/norm/index.htm (International Labour Organization Labour Standards)

www.un.org/Overview/rights.html (Universal Declaration of Human Rights)

A sustainable day

How could you make your day more sustainable?

Achieving a sustainable society depends on people making choices that help to promote a sustainable world. This means that we must learn both to choose to take actions that support sustainable lifestyles and refuse to undertake those that don't.

Consider how your day started. What did you have for breakfast?

Did the food and drink you enjoyed come from local sources, or had it been brought a long way to your home village, town or city

by plane or boat? How did you get to school? Did you walk or use a bicycle? Or did you use public transport where the energy used is shared among many people? Or perhaps someone made a special journey to get you there?

Inspirational products

Electric bicycles have become much more successful in recent years, and many people believe that is because they have designed to be more stylish and more fun.

For information about electric bicycles & examples of designs that help people to decide to adopt the new technology, see:

www.50cycles.com
www.sbsb.co.uk
www.urbanmover.com
www.verteci.com

Torq electric hybrid
(www.50cycles.com)

E-Cycle - with NiMH Battery
(www.verteci.com)

The Sakura Mustang
(www.sbsb.co.uk)

UM70SX Surfer
(www.urbanmover.com)

Activities

- Discuss with your friends how you live and list some actions you could take, and some that you could refuse to take, in order to help make the world more sustainable.

- Form small teams and develop a product proposal for a 'Dragon's Den' like the TV show. Each dragon should wear an 'economic', 'environmental', or 'social' hat and, if you have time, you should make real hats to help the dragons get into their roles. Then, taking turns to be dragons, interrogate the product proposers and refuse to support any that they cannot defend on sustainability grounds.

- Sketch out ideas for posters which would help other students to reconsider their lifestyles.

- Complete a booklet showing a day in your life now and some actions that you could take and refuse to take in order to promote a more sustainable lifestyle.

- Take something from the booklet you have made and redesign it for your major project.

For more information visit:

www.biothinking.com/storyof.htm
(Edwin Datschefski describes his
story of a sustainable day on his
website. Reading it should help you to
remember some of the things you need
to think about, or read his book, *The
Total Beauty of Sustainable Products*,
published by RotoVision in 2001.)

Unfair fashion

Are cheap clothes sustainable?

Clothing prices are now so low that shoppers are treating their clothes as practically disposable!
But who pays the cost of cheap clothes?

One of the factors allowing UK retailers to sell clothes cheaply is low production costs. In many of the countries where value retailers source clothing, huge savings are made through low wages. Average hourly wages in 2000 were 0.46 in China, £0.38 in India, and £0.13 in Sri Lanka (calculated on 2005 exchange rate).
(www.corporatewatch.org.uk)

Make me fair

• Design a product (or a range) for a fashion company with fair trade values.

Activities

• Ask students to bring in two pieces of clothing from home (or use their school uniforms). In groups, do a quick label check to see where their clothes were made. Do all companies tell you where their clothes were made? If not, why is this?

• Encourage students to think what information they would like to see about a product on the label or packaging. Develop an eco-labelling example to let shoppers have information about how and where they were made.

• What does fair trade mean? Find some logos that may be used to claim that a garment has been fairly traded.

• Look at a fair trade T-shirt and compare it to a T-shirt bought in a local supermarket or from a catalogue that does not claim to be fairly traded. Evaluate the two products using the 'Winners and losers' tool in section 5.

Textiles

Sustainable schools doorways

8

For more information, see:

For KS3/4 view www.stepin.org/index.php?id=ft_context
(fair trade fashion brief)

For AS/A2 view www.sda-uk.org/tx5.html
(fair trade design context)

Fair trade

How can textile design help those living in poverty?

In 2006, the world's Football Association made over £200m from sponsorship and licensing, while the sponsors were able to make millions of pounds in additional income from World Cup goods.

People sewing the shirts, stitching balls and gluing the boots worked late into the night, six or seven days a week, for poverty wages. Some people who attempted to improve their working conditions were persecuted or lost their jobs. (www.labourbehindthelabel.org)

These facts aren't here to make you feel guilty for buying them, but to raise issues and point to alternatives!

Fair trade footballs are produced in Sialkot, a small town in the Punjab in Pakistan, where thousands of children work in the football production industry.

The supplier of fair trade footballs – Talon Sports – has to register all stitchers and their ages, so they can ensure they are not employing under-age workers.

Because they are paid a fair wage, families can afford to send their children to school instead of to work.

A 'social premium' is also paid, which supports childcare, education, and credit schemes – so that the whole community benefits from fair trade.

Fair trade fashion

People Tree is a fair trade fashion company which works closely with producer groups to design stylish, high quality products that are ecologically manufactured and make good use of traditional skills and technologies. The clothes are dyed using low impact dyes, free from harmful azo chemicals frequently used in clothing manufacture. The company uses locally available and natural materials where possible and actively avoids plastics and toxic substances.

Assisi Garments is a producer group for People Tree based in India. Employees benefit from training, fair wages, a lump sum paid after five years' employment to start a home, and a clean, safe and supportive working environment.

Activities

- Visit a sports shop/look in catalogues and find out where sports equipment and garments are made
- Find out more about fair trade issues in sportswear
- What can people do if they want to protest against unfair working conditions for people involved in making sportswear?
- Research into any sportswear that has been fairly traded and compare this with non fair trade products (cost, quality etc). You could use the evaluation tools (Design abacus or Eco-web in Section 5) to help you.

Make me fairer

Develop a range of products for a fair trade sportswear company. Don't forget to include labelling that conveys the message you want shoppers to get.

For more information visit:

www.peopletree.co.uk (fair trade fashion)

www.oxfam.org.uk ('Looking behind the Logo' is a role-play activity about working conditions for those in the sportswear Industry)

www.labourbehindthelabel.org (information on fair trade campaigns for KS4 and 16+)

www.stepin.org (eco-fashion case study)

www.katherinehamnett.com (fashion designer and environmental campaigner)

Throwaway drinks containers

How can we avoid throwing away so much?

We often use throwaway drink containers. These usually end up in landfill – or even as litter! This is a waste of materials. Recycling the materials takes energy and causes pollution, and cannot take away the impact of making the object in the first place.

In many universities in Canada and Germany, students are given a reusable cup. If they bring it to buy drinks in the cafeteria, they pay much less. Cafes on railway stations will put a drink in your own cup. You can now buy stainless steel mugs with a lid. In some places you can still find a water fountain.

Reusable plastic mugs that keep cold drinks cold and hot drinks hot are sold by the Arizona Student Unions to encourage waste reduction. Refills in these mugs are given at a reduced price at Student Union operated food outlets located around campus.

(www.recycledproductsonline.co.uk)

Activities

Working in groups, look at a variety of drink containers such as:

- Plastic bottles
- Tetra Paks
- Tea/coffee take-away cups
- Plastic sachets
- Cans
- Water cooler cups

Discuss: How many of them could we REFUSE to use, yet still have the drink?

Make me low impact

Design and model a system for low impact drinks.

What materials are they?

- Think about bottled water. Health experts are now worried about contamination from the plastic to the bottle.
  Tap water has legal standards of minerals etc.
  Bottled water manufacturers do not have to put a chemical or bacteriological analysis on their bottles.
  Why don't we use tap water?

- What about the cups of coffee on those long train journeys? Can we do that without a throwaway cup?

- What about fizzy drinks etc? What are the ingredients? Are they better for us than water?

For more information visit:
www.vitalgraphics.net/waste/

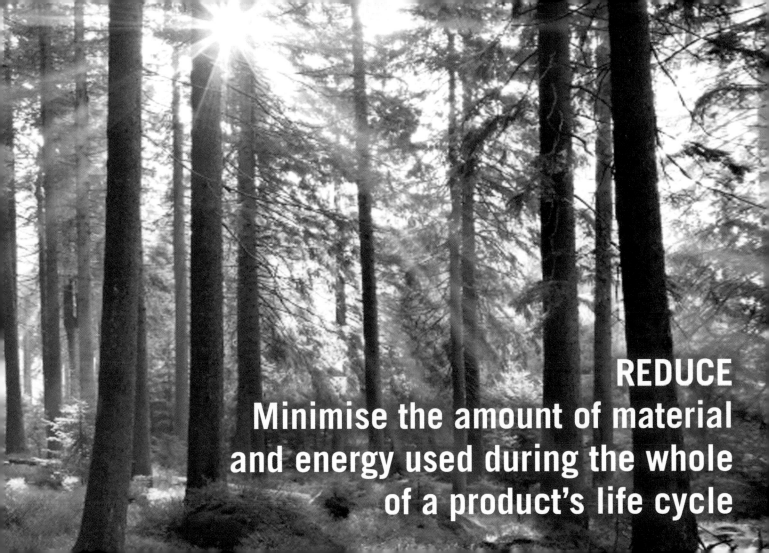

REDUCE
Minimise the amount of material and energy used during the whole of a product's life cycle

Where's the impact?

What are the impacts of a product through its life cycle?

We often overlook the impact products have after they have been produced. Analysing the whole product life cycle can help us to find ways of minimising our footprint.

Work out your own footprint at http://footprint.wwf.org.uk/

Facts

- If everyone used the world's available productive land equally, we would each have about **1.8 hectares.**
- That's about **three senior football pitches** (100 x 60 metres)
- In the UK we currently use over **5 hectares** each…
- That means we're using THREE times our share of the world's resources.

(www.cat.org.uk)

Activity

In this activity students analyse consumer items and think about all stages of their production and what it involved in energy and land use. They work out the life cycle of the product from start to finish. They can then discuss the impact of any product on the environment and on other people.

- Students work in groups using a set of cards that represent the stages of production, use and disposal of any consumer item. Examples of the sorts of cards are illustrated here.

- The activity works best with products which students can disassemble to identify component parts, or where ingredients are identified on a label, e.g. a can of soft drink.

- Ask students to identify every field, factory, lorry, ship, landfill etc. that would be used in the product's life cycle.

Ready-to-use copies of the activity can be obtained from the Centre for Alternative Technology (www.cat.org.uk/edresources)

Suitable for all D&T areas

Sustainable schools doorways

 2 3
 4 8

For more information visit:

A fuller description of this activity is given in the DFES Key Stage 3 Strategy document, p 319-322.

www.panda.org/livingplanet/ (background information)

www.sei.se/reap/download_login. php?region=l (about your area)

http://footprint.wwf.org.uk/

Product pairs

How can we reduce materials and energy use?

We are able to obtain different versions of one product, e.g. glass or plastic coke bottle, real or artificial Christmas tree, battery-powered or hand-operated fan, but how often do we consider the social, economic and environmental impacts of the alternatives?

The product pairs activity encourages students to do so.

Inspirational product

This toothbrush design uses the person's finger as the shank, reducing the amount of materials and energy consumed.

Activity

Work in groups. Each group is given different pair of products with the same function but different materials. They need to know how to use the Design abacus or Eco-design web (described later in this book) to compare the two products. Consider:

- Material type (all component materials)
- Manufacturing methods
- Renewable/ non-renewable materials
- Refillable
- Energy use
- Cost
- Packaging
- Disassembly
- Weight - transport
- Where manufactured?
- Exploitation
- Is it recyclable?

Introduce areas that need to be investigated - give example questions such as 'What is it made of?' and 'How is it manufactured?' Get students to come up with more questions. Findings could be displayed as a poster - show the impacts of the products. Can you tell which is best?

Redesign me

What improvements can students suggest? Different materials? New design that uses less energy?

all D&T areas

Sustainable schools doorways

For more information visit:

www.stepin.org

www.informationinspiration.org.uk

Unhealthy food

What is the impact of food products on your health?

A balanced, healthy diet

If people have a balanced diet over a week, they are far less likely to get heart disease, diabetes, osteoporosis, diverticulitis, appendicitis, and some cancers.

The first step to a balanced diet is to eat 5 pieces of fruit and vegetables each day.

REDUCE the amount of salt, sugar and fat for a more sustainable lifestyle. Make sure you have enough fibre, vitamins and minerals. Processed foods usually contain more salt, sugar and fat and, with red meat and dairy products, have a high impact on the planet. Increased portion size is likely to lead to even more wastage than there is already.

Facts

- In Britain we throw away £20 billion worth of unused food every year (the *Independent*, 15 April, 2005)
- Over the past 30 years, manufactured foodstuff portions have increased by up to a half. For example, a packet of crisps now contains 35 grams compared with 25 g then.
- Pizza sizes are growing (28 cm instead of 25).
- One supermarket's standard shepherd's pie contains 5.9 g salt per portion – the total daily recommended intake is only 6 g.
- Guideline Daily Amounts (GDA) are given on nutrition panels.

Activities

- Discuss why we buy so much processed food. Why don't people cook at home as much as they used to? Why does processed food have a bigger environmental impact? Is home cooking fun?

- Carry out a product analysis on portion sizes of ready-cooked meals.

- Investigate how much rice or pasta you need to cook for one portion.

- Weigh the amount of food you throw away at home in the next week – add together for a class total.

Make me tasty

- Adapt a pizza and a spaghetti bolognese recipe to have reduced fat and salt. Conduct a taste experiment to see if others can tell the difference.

- Make reduced-sugar biscuits by using alternatives like dried or fresh fruit.

- Produce a poster on portion size for a variety of foodstuffs (pasta, rice, vegetables, chicken) to encourage others to think about how much they need.

- Design a 'Get the balance right' leaflet for primary school children.

Food technology

Sustainable schools doorways

 1 2 4

For more information visit:
www.5aday.nhs.uk
www.bbc.co.uk/health
www.theleanteam.co.uk
www.teenweightwise.com
www.realbuzz.com

Energy use

How can we reduce energy use in food technology?

Sustainability in food must mostly be about food! It is too easy to think that if we recycle packaging we have done our bit where food is concerned. A lot of energy is used in the processing, transporting and cooking of food.

The eco-footprint of beef and dairy products is high. The production, transport and refrigeration of each pound of meat in the UK leads to around 4.7 kg CO2 equivalent. (www.coinet.org.uk)

One lettuce from California takes 60 times more energy to transport than you get from eating it. (*I Count: Your step-by-step guide to climate bliss,* Penguin.)

'One of the biggest household energy guzzlers is the very thing few of us could countenance life without: the kettle.

The energy used to boil one kettle of water could light a room for an entire evening. On top of that, most of us heat more water than we need and sometimes boil kettles more than once before actually making that cup of tea.' (BBC)

Inspirational product

The kambrook axis kettle is designed to reduce the amount of water and energy used when boiling a kettle.
For more info see www. informationinspiration.org

Activities

- Discuss whether we consider energy use enough when planning the making of food products.
  - Do you use an oven to cook just one product?
  - Do you use food processors and mixers more than necessary?
  - Do you avoid over-filling or re-boiling kettles?
  - Do you make use of pressure cookers or slow cookers where possible?

- Include an analysis of energy use in all evaluations.
- Look at disposable products - cutlery and plates and also disposable barbecues. Are they sustainable? How much energy is saved with washing up or making a longer-lasting product?

- Analyse a traditional roast dinner - instead of the oven and four hobs being used, use just the oven. Or, for a lemon meringue pie, work out how you can reduce the energy of using a whisk, hob and oven (3 times).

- Analyse the life cycle of a product and work out how to reduce the energy used to make that product - see 'Where's the Impact?' resource from www.cat.org.uk/edresources, and use a pizza, kinder egg, Indian takeaway.

- Learn traditional and basic skills in food preparation such as chopping herbs, slicing potatoes, hand beating egg whites so that electrical equipment is not used.

Make me uncooked

Design a range of products that use as many raw ingredients as possible to reduce the use of energy - for example, vegetable salads, dips and raw vegetables, fruit salads, fruit smoothies, fruit and vegetable juices.

Food technology

Sustainable schools doorways

Personal energy meter

How much energy do you use in a week?

Most of the electrical energy we use is generated from coal, gas or oil, which are carbon-based, and this adds to climate change. In order to reduce CO_2 emission from these fuels, we need to use less energy. For example, in the UK, the estimated energy wasted by leaving computers switched on when they are not being used is 1 million Watts per hour, or one power station.

Facts

• Using the washing line instead of the tumble dryer saves 1.5 kg CO_2 per use.

• 'We use £1.3 billion worth of electricity by using washing machines, tumble dryers and dishwashers. This produces 5m tonnes (equivalent to 32 million double decker buses) of CO_2 each year.' (Energy Savings Trust)

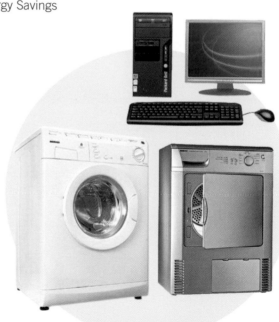

Activities

- For one week, students keep a daily record of how long they use electrical appliances. This is their personal energy meter.

- Record use of electrical appliances on a spreadsheet. Students can create their own spreadsheet or they can download a template from Microsoft's Personal Energy Meter website.

- Find out the power rating, measured in Watts, of the appliances used. Remember electrical safety: students must ask an adult to help find the appliance's rating label. The Energy Guide website will help if the rating is not easy to find.

- Use the personal energy meter and the appliance power ratings to work out the amount of electricity used and the cost.

- Analyse use of energy and identify ways to save it. Visit the Energy Hog website for ideas to help.

- Repeat the personal energy meter for another week, using as many ways as possible to save energy. Try involving family and friends to do the same.

- How much energy have you saved in a week?

- Students produce a poster for others to follow their lead.

Sustainable schools
doorways

For more information visit:

www.energyhog.org
(improving energy efficiency)

A sustainable school

What are the issues that sustainable designers should think about?

Sustainability is easier to achieve if school buildings are designed with energy use in mind. However, everyday objects such as pens, rulers and other equipment can also be designed and used in more or less sustainable ways. Schools use materials that could be recycled, and have many groups of people that need to be included within the drive towards greater sustainability.

Product story

An interesting example of a product where the appropriate approach to sustainable design is unclear is a pen or biro. The most common Bic biros are made from recyclable polymers, they are low cost so that everyone can afford them, and they last quite a long time. However, because they are cheap, people tend to take them for granted and many of them are thrown away or lost before they are fully used. Designers have thought about this, and produced biodegradable pens from corn starch, pens made from recycled polymers, wooden pens and pens with 30 miles of ink, which have been designed to last a lifetime. But how is it possible to decide on the best approach?

Green Flower Ballpen from the Green Pen Company. Biodegradable capped ballpen made from corn starch with a seed pod attached containing Aster seeds that can be planted.

The Space Pen Millennium 2k edition has a lifetime's worth of ink (30 miles), so it's the only pen you'll ever need, if you don't lose it! (from www.biothinking.com)

(www.cat.org.uk)

Make me with less

- Create a poster which illustrates sustainability issues that a designer should take into account in considering the design of an everyday product.

- Plan an exhibition of products showing how sustainability could be improved (e.g. for the school foyer or Design and Technology department, or a point-of-sale display).

Activities

- Take an everyday product (e.g. a pen, mobile phone) and write down all the issues which the designers and makers of the product should have considered.

- Capture images relating to sustainability around your school and discuss the most sustainable ways of capturing and storing such images (each student could use different tools, e.g. digital cameras, film-based cameras, disposable cameras, sketching, notes).

For more information visit:

www.informationinspiration.org.uk (things that designers should be thinking about)

www.remarkable.co.uk/ (pencils and other very interesting products)

www.greenpens.co.uk/ (many different approaches)

Waste

How can textile designers reduce waste?

The fashion industry, with its interest in designing fashion garments for just one season, contributes towards the high volume of textiles waste.

In the UK, we throw away one million tonnes of textiles each year. The production of these textiles has used energy and resources, caused pollution and often involved exploitation of people who produce them.

The best option for textiles (above reuse and recycling) is waste reduction. By that we mean *make less stuff!* This would involve less material being used, so reducing the impact on the environment.

One way of achieving this is to challenge the new fast-fashion fad, encouraging designers to develop products that will stand the test of time (in terms of both durability and style).

In addition, designers should consider whether their products can be easily and cost effectively reused and recycled at their end of life.

Most lightweight cotton twill trousers are made from two-fold cotton. Howies', on the other hand, are made from three-fold cotton which makes them a little harder wearing, to last a bit longer.

Inspirational product

(www.howies.co.uk)

Make me last longer

Design a textiles product that will stand the test of time.

Activities

- Think of products made from textiles in your home. Which ones have lasted the longest?
- What features do they have?
- Investigate design classics: which designs and materials stand the test of time? Ask older relatives, look at photos, look back through fashion magazines to see the clothing that has come back into fashion.
- Research how designers forecast future fashions.

- Encourage students to forecast fashion in Year 7/8 and then place the forecasts in a Time Capsule to open when they're in Year 10/11. How accurate were they?
- Know your materials: some materials and construction techniques give harder-wearing properties.
- Look at a range of garments (photos will do!) and sketch ideas of how they could be altered to keep up with trends rather than throwing them away.

Textiles

Sustainable schools doorways

4

For more information visit:

www.sda-org.uk
(materials and durability)

www.howies.co.uk (environmentally sound fashion company)

Costing the Earth?

How can we reduce the impact of textiles over their life cycle?

Many of the UK's value retailers are selling jeans for as little as £3. It's estimated that Tesco alone sells 30,000 pairs a week.

Few of us living in the UK today are aware of the long journey of textile products from design to eventual disposal. The impact of the product on people involved in production and on the environment will depend largely on choice of material (fibre and fabric), production methods (including dyeing and finishing), use and care of the product, transportation and eventual disposal.

Facts

Printing is one of the most complex areas in textiles production. The dyeing of textiles has been dominated by the use of synthetic dyes. Recently natural dyes have become popular because of the health and environmental concerns associated with synthetic dyes.

Washing and drying clothes has a relatively high environmental impact, associated with the use of water and fossil fuels to generate electricity for heating water and air for laundering clothes.

Tumble dryers are the most energy-consuming appliances in the home. So, get into the habit of thinking about your use of electricity and start hanging your clothes up to dry, and avoid ironing where possible!

A single washing machine cycle uses roughly 100 litres of water per cycle. How many washes does your family do per week? Calculate your annual consumption of water.

Many of us wash clothes after a single use (even when they don't appear dirty!). Think twice about putting your clothes for washing and experiment with using a lower temperature to save energy.

Inspirational product

Alisa Cordon's A-level project – a dress made for a boutique to promote sustainable textiles. (www.sda-uk.org)

Sustainable schools doorways

Activities

- Using any textile product of interest to students, carry out a life cycle analysis. You may wish to use picture cards (from 'Where's the impact?' activity earlier in this section) and use the headings of Fibres and fabric production, Dyeing and printing, Marketing and sale of product, Use of product and Disposal.

- Where in the product life cycle could you make environmental improvements in the production and manufacturing of the textiles product?

- Check out the websites www.nosweat.org.uk and www.labourbehindthelabel.org to enable you to find out where people are affected in the life cycle of your product.

- Check out an electrical appliance's efficiency to find out how much water and energy it needs. Some of the more efficient appliances use up to 50% less water.

For more information visit:

www.greenbuildingstore.co.uk

www.environmentagency.co.uk/savewater

www.sda-uk.org/materials (for information on advantages and disadvantages of natural and synthetic materials)

www.practicalaction.org/practicalanswers (for technical information on use of natural dyes)

www.corporatewatch.org.uk (hourly rates paid to garment workers).

The newspaper bridge

How can we maintain fitness for purpose while minimising material use?

If we continue to use building materials in the way we do now, it has been estimated that we will need by 2050:

- 6 planets worth of steel
- 3.5 planets for cement supply
- 3.5 planets to meet timber demand.

We cannot sustain such overuse of resources, so we should try to design in a way that minimises resource use while maintaining fitness for purpose.

Make me with less

The task is to build a bridge from newspaper and sticky labels that will span an agreed distance between two desks (e.g. 30-40 cm) and which will support an agreed weight (e.g. 100 g). The winner will be the person or team whose bridge supports the weight for 5 minutes with the least amount of paper and fewest labels. Only the prescribed materials, including paper, can be used. You can vary these yourself, bearing sustainability in mind.

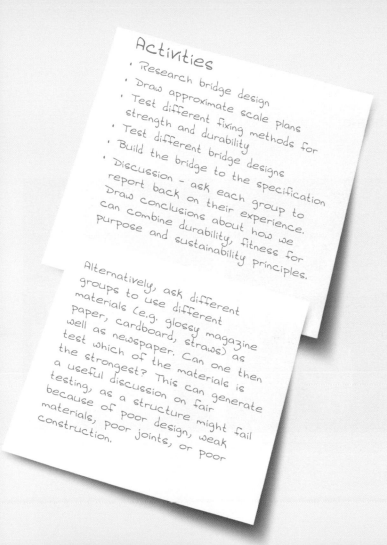

Activities

- Research bridge design
- Draw approximate scale plans
- Test different fixing methods for strength and durability
- Test different bridge designs
- Build the bridge to the specification
- Discussion – ask each group to report back on their experience. Draw conclusions about how we can combine durability, fitness for purpose and sustainability principles.

Alternatively, ask different groups to use different materials (e.g. glossy magazine paper, cardboard, straws) as well as newspaper. Can one then test which of the materials is the strongest? This can generate a useful discussion on fair testing, as a structure might fail because of poor design, weak materials, poor joints, or poor construction.

Problem

To achieve a fair test the load must be put on each bridge in an identical way – preferably placed very gently in the middle. This can be used to generate discussion on the difference between static loads and dynamic or live loads, and why engineers need to build in substantial safety margins. The sustainability challenge is to make a safe bridge with adequate margins for different conditions, using minimum materials, minimum embodied energy and design for ease of maintenance.

For more information visit:

www.exploratorium.org/structures/newspaper.html

www.design-technology.org/bridges.htm

Shopping bags

How do you get your shopping home?

Facts

Plastic carrier bags are made from LDPE or sometimes from PP. Both of these are made from oil – although occasionally they are made from recycled plastics. They can take up to 500 years to decay in landfill.

We could use paper bags, but these are much heavier and therefore use more fuel to transport them to the shop, and they break easily when they become wet.

An obvious alternative is a reusable bag, made maybe from organically sourced, fair-traded hemp or cotton. This is far better than using throw-away plastic bags. But driving to do the shopping will have a much bigger impact than the type of bag. Is there an alternative?

Make me car-free

Design a bag or trolley that helps a fashion-conscious young person to shop without the car. What low impact materials could you make a shopping trolley from?

Would you be seen with one of these?

Sustainable schools doorways

3 **4**

For more information:

www.stepin.org/casestudy.php?id=bicycletrailers
(case study on multi-purpose bike trailers)

www.sda-uk.org (throwaway culture: shopping bags)

www.traid.org.uk (Say no to plastic bags!)

www.canby.co.uk (hemp and organic cotton bags)

REUSE

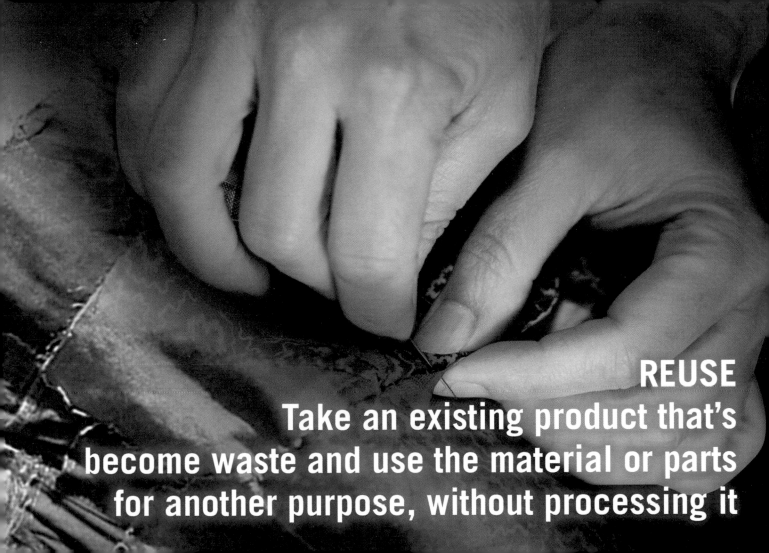

REUSE
Take an existing product that's become waste and use the material or parts for another purpose, without processing it

The reuse challenge

Reusing does less harm than recycling, since products do not have to be processed before they can be used.

Waste facts

What's your waste measurement?

Average UK person throws away

- 450 kg of waste every year
- 149 kg of paper and card
  (= 570 *Radio Times*)
- 90 kg organic stuff
  (= 2,000 banana skins)
- 50 kg plastics
  (= 900 fizzy drink bottles)
- 32 kg metals
  (= 630 baked bean tins)

A Chinese child sits in the middle of a pile of e-waste. Children are among the workers who dismantle discarded computers, printers, TVs and other e-waste, containing many hazardous chemicals. (Greenpeace)

Discuss: Is this what REUSE should be about? Dumping in less-developed countries... Or these examples of inspirational products?

Inspirational products

Danielle Benbow's award-winning chair made from carpet rolls and magazines.

▶

Refillable printer ink cartridges.

▼

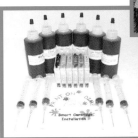

Plastic bag pouffe. Knitted and crocheted from plastic carrier bags

▶

Activities

- Ask students to bring in examples of stuff that is regularly thrown away – e.g. yoghurt pots, vegetable trays, crisp packets, or plastic bags. Bring in some examples of your own.

- Divide the class into groups. Give each group something from the scrap bin.

- Ask them to brainstorm different ways in which the product might be reused. Pass products round until each group has had each product.

- Report back and discuss reuse!

How much waste?

Collect all the rubbish from your tutor room every day for a week. Separate it into different types, weigh it and work out your yearly waste (e.g. paper, plastic, glass).

Sustainable schools doorways

For more information visit:
www.wasteonline.org.uk
www.greenpeace.org

Leftover food

Can we make use of leftover food?

Britain throws away £20 billion worth of unused food every year – equal to five times our spending on international aid and enough to lift 150 million people out of starvation (*The Independent* 15.03.05). When food waste ends up in a landfill site, it rots and produces methane, which is a powerful greenhouse gas.

If food waste cannot be reused, it can be recycled in a compost heap, to produce useful fertiliser for your garden.

It is easy to reuse other materials such as textiles, but there are often hygiene issues with leftover foods. A lot of traditional ways with leftover foods have been lost in today's busy lifestyles: boiling a chicken carcass to make soup or mincing up the leftover roast beef to make cottage pie or rissoles.

This might be the time to revive those skills.

Inspirational products

Respect Organics make a range of organic cakes including banana cake. They are able to use bananas rejected by supermarkets as not the right quality – over-ripe or damaged – as they need very ripe bananas for their cakes and it doesn't matter if parts are bruised as they will be cut off before going into the cake mixture. Respect are able to obtain these bananas at a good price because they are in effect reusing waste materials – no one else wanted them!

(www.respectorganics.co.uk)

Activities

Analyse a Christmas dinner, its leftovers and how they can be used. Carry out focused tasks with particular leftover ingredients such as sprouts and potatoes or turkey. Research different recipes on the internet.

Make me

Make croquettes using cooked meat, cooked vegetables and cooked potatoes or rice. Use home-made dried breadcrumbs. Use Spanish tapas recipes for a variety of croquettes. Oven bake to reduce the fat content.

Have a practical project around a roast chicken, cut off the meat to be used for that meal. Plan and make t least two more meals with the leftovers, e.g. curry, soup, risotto, croquettes. Include a lesson on the hygiene issues of using leftover foods.

Sustainable schools doorways

1 **4**

For more information visit:

www.frugalliving.about.com

WEEE and you

Can we make more use of dismantled electrical parts?

At present, the UK produces over one million tonnes of waste electrical and electronic equipment every year, or three tonnes per British citizen in their lifetime. On 1 January 2006, manufacturers and retailers in the European Union became responsible for financing the collection of ten categories of product at the end of their life cycle – though implementation of this legislation was delayed in the UK. The legislation covering this is the European Waste from Electrical and Electronic Equipment (WEEE) Directive. Article 4 of this

Directive, 'Product Design', encourages 'the design and production of electrical and electronic equipment which take into account and facilitate dismantling and recovery, in particular the reuse and recycling of WEEE, their components and materials.'

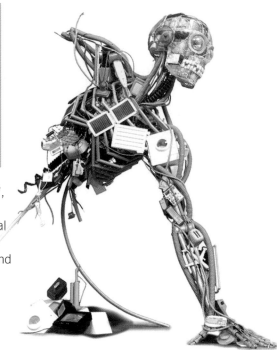

Inspirational product

Kodak single use cameras are collected and many parts are reused.

Sustainable schools doorways

Activities

- Visit the WEEEman and the Wasteonline websites to find out more about the WEEE Directive, the ten categories of electrical and electronic waste, and design and disposal.

- Brainstorm economic and environmental issues about dismantling products for recycling and reuse of their components. Students should be made aware of the difference between recycling and reuse.

- Encourage students to reuse components in their designing and making from irreparable products and from unwanted school projects. Students should report how they have reused components in their designs, including the economic and environmental impact of their actions.

- Develop design and make activities that rely entirely on reuse of electronic and electrical components, including parts for their cases.

For more information see:

www.wasteonline.org.uk (information sheets)

www.weeeman.org (design and disposal of electrical products)

www.informationinspiration.org.uk

REUSE

Packaging

How can packaging promote sustainable design?

Packaging is necessary for many products. Its design, and the logos and trademarks used on it, can give people important messages about the source and quality of products. Packaging is also seen as symptomatic of a consumerist society, and logos and brand identity are disliked by many as the symbols of large corporations.

However, it is possible to use these powerful tools and symbols of consumerism to support and promote more sustainable lifestyles. These activities are about taking the powerful images created for advertising, and the clever packaging designs used in the distribution of products, and reusing them in the sustainability cause.

Inspirational products

Lily Trotter designed and made a reusable peanut butter container for a women's group in Nakuru, Kenya. The jar was designed with the collaboration of the women and can be reused as a drinks container. If you are designing for a group it is essential to have feedback on your ideas and project from those you are designing for.

Lily was able to get this support for her work through the Sustainable Design Awards.

If you are interested in pursuing this kind of project, then you should consider contacting Practical Action to see if they are able to help you.

This poster designed for the Body Shop promotes sustainability.

Tinkertown Museum, Alburque, New Mexico has glass bottle walls made of 55,000 bottles, which took over 15 years to construct

Activities

- Create a poster showing products that need packaging.

- Bring in examples of packaging and discuss whether the packaging currently used is too much or too little. Can you show how the amount of packaging could be reduced?

- Collect 20 logos and/or trademarks and discuss what they communicate to the customer.

- Choose one of the six 'R's used in this pack and create the letters in a new format by reusing logos or trademarks in an intriguing way.

Make me worthwhile

- Redesign packaging for reuse, so that it becomes a desirable item for the product purchaser to treasure or collect.

- It has been decided that a new set of stamps is to be designed which promote sustainability in society. Design six stamps for this purpose by reusing images developed to promote consumerism.

- Reuse necessary packaging in designing products to help your school be more sustainable. Staples, and toxic glues and inks should be avoided.

- Redesign the packaging of a product so that it becomes its own point of sale display.

Graphics

Sustainable schools doorways

 4 8

For more information visit:
www.sda-uk.org/
www.bodyshop.co.uk

TRAID remade

How can used textiles be reused in new products?

Facts

- Textiles make up around 4% of household waste in Europe.

- Only 25% is reused in some way, with 75% going to landfill.

- In the UK the most common reuse of textiles is organised by charity shops.

- Most charity shops will resell your clothes/textiles in the UK or, where the items are too worn, pass them on to be reused (for wiping cloths in industry) or recycled for use for furniture filling and/or insulation material.

Textile Recycling for Aid and International Development (TRAID) is one organisation reusing over 2,500 tonnes of textiles each year.

From clothes collected at one of the 700 banks around the UK, designers at TRAID redesign and make a range of clothing for sale in their shops.

The challenge for designers is to use what's available to come up with marketable products.

Often a garment is re-cut and reconstructed to make something completely new.

TRAID designers use a combination of traditional craft techniques through to graphics and printing techniques to create contemporary clothing.

Inspirational products

The clipper shoulder bag is made from the decommissioned sail of a yacht. (www.ecocentric.co.uk)

Activities

Encourage students to think about what happens to textiles in their homes when they are finished with.

Make me desirable

- Design and make a usable product from 'waste' textiles.
- Design a marketable product for a store such as TRAID Remade.

Textiles

Sustainable schools doorways

For more information visit:

www.kettex.com

www.traid.org.uk (Textile Recycling for Aid & Development)

www.foe.co.uk (Friends of the Earth)

www.stepin.org.uk (KS3 or 4 scheme of work on related brief, KS3 research project on Waste to Wear)

www.sda-uk.org (AS/A2 textiles briefs)

www.ecocentric.co.uk

www.biothinking.com (other inspirational products, including fashion & furnishings from reclaimed materials)

Small products

How can 'waste' be transformed into useful and/or beautiful products?

Many small products are so plentiful and thought to be so insignificant that they are often thrown away without any thought. Were they useful in the first place? Should they have been made at all?

Given that they do exist, and often in large quantities, are they really waste or can they be made into something useful?

Inspirational product

Katie Chapman, when she was a student at Beaconsfield High School, found loads of photographic slides at her grandparents' house. She realised that many people had lots of similar slides lying around – families, friends, pets, buildings, scenery, flowers etc. She had the idea of making her family slides into a lampshade. In her father's workshop she found lots of metal

washers and used them to join the slides. In the project she also used an old saucepan lid, a shower rail, coat hangers, a mobile phone charger and gauze to make a lamp stand.

A-level students Kirstie Nicholls and Emma Berry both developed methods for reusing a variety of materials to produce packaging products.

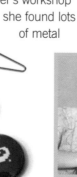

Activities

- Write down as many items as the class can think of which are regularly thrown away as useless - lollipop sticks, bottle tops, plastic bottles, ring can pulls, electric cables, sweet papers, crisp packets, coat hangers, buttons, aluminium foil, cartons, toilet roll inserts, etc.

- Discuss whether or not there are some items that it is OK to throw away. How do you decide?

- Are there any things thrown away in the D&T department that could be reused?

- Work in small groups. Choose three or more items that are frequently thrown away. List products they could make using little or no processing or recycling.

Re-make me

- Students will make a light-up key fob from a 'sandwich' of reused material which might previously have been regarded as waste at home or school. It will also have an LED circuit built into it.

- They will need the following resources - string, card, plastic (from home), sign-maker's vinyl, rubber (mouse mats), battery (long-lasting or rechargeable?), LED circuit including something for making a switch

- Design a recycle promotion logo to go onto the fob.
- Mark and cut the rubber or neoprene or whatever is being used.
- Make a hole for the battery
- Mark and cut the card or plastic
- Stick together using non-toxic method
- Vinyl cut logo (CAD-CAM possibilities)
- Add string 'chain'.

Product design

For more information visit:

www.sda-uk.org

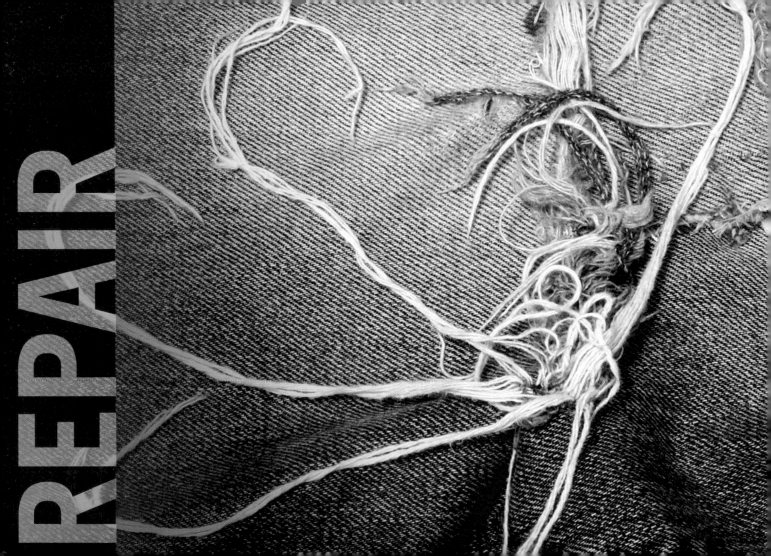

REPAIR

REPAIR
When a product breaks down or doesn't function properly, fix it

Disassemble me (if you can)

Do we care if we don't repair?

Facts

• Every year, we throw away about 1 million tonnes of textile waste in the UK. At least 50% are recyclable, and many items could be repaired. How many people patch or darn?

• We also throw away over 1 million tonnes of electrical equipment, especially computers and televisions. What do we do if our iPod breaks down? Do we try to get it repaired or hope we can afford a new one? See www.vitalgraphics.net/ for where they end up.

Inspired design

These shoes, made by Trippen in Germany, are designed so the rubber sole can be easily removed from the upper to make the soles either exchangeable or recyclable.

How many products are designed to be repaired?

Activities

• Ask your grandparents about the things they used to repair but which people no longer think about repairing. Try to find out from them if they know what the following products are – a last, a mushroom, a kilner jar, a Box Brownie, a Ewbank cleaner.... (see opposite page)

• Discuss what manufacturers want you to do – repair or buy a new one?

• Investigate everyday electrical items such as coffee makers or electric toothbrushes. See if you think they have been made so that they can be repaired.

For more information visit:
www.vitalgraphics.net/
(Vital Waste Graphics pp36-37,
Vital Waste Graphics 2 p22)

www.wasteonline.org.uk

Kitchen equipment

Should there be a scheme to repair electrical equipment?

There are lots of discussions and articles about 'computer mountains' – thrown away after just a few years of use. There are even schemes where these computers are repaired and sent to developing countries. What about the waste fridges and kettles, and all the other kitchen electrical equipment?

How many pieces of electrical equipment have you and your family thrown away this past year?

Should there be a scheme to repair different electrical equipment? What is needed to enable this to be done and the repaired equipment reused?

What can you do to reduce the number of times you use electrical equipment so that it lasts longer?

'I threw a travel kettle into the bin in my hotel room on holiday in Kenya. It had a crack down the side so I could only boil a little water at a time. The next day, one of the hotel workers knocked on the bedroom door and asked if I could sign a document to say that I had thrown it away. His bag would be searched when he finished his shift and without this document he would be accused of stealing. He couldn't afford a new kettle - they were too expensive on his wage.
He could easily mend this and use it.'
Lesley Woods

Activities

- Choose 10 different pieces of kitchen electrical equipment. Put them in order of priority of use. Choose two you couldn't do without and justify this choice. Choose four that you could easily do without.

- Investigate the history of the electric kettle and its use in other countries. How was water heated before the electric kettle?

- Take one of the products and redesign it so it can be repaired.

Food technology

Sustainable schools doorways

For more information visit:

www.npower.com/At_home/Go_green.html
(energy used in the home by different appliances)

www.vitalgraphics.net/waste/
(Vital Waste Graphics 2 p20, 21, 22 & 30)

Fix it!

Is new always best anywhere in the house or at school?

Unwanted electronic and electrical equipment is growing three times faster than any other waste category. This includes many items that could be repaired easily. There is a need to encourage a culture of repair rather than replace when products stop working. However, many items can be repaired only by the suitably qualified or experienced. A good starting point is to teach young people the appropriate skills of fault-finding and repair.

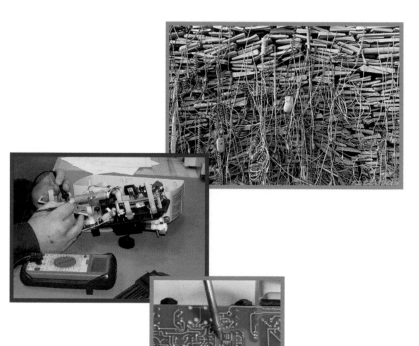

Activities

- Find out more about repair, reuse and recycling of electronic and electrical equipment.
- Collect electrical products that no longer work - for safety reasons, only battery-powered items, not mains-powered. Remove batteries before attempting repair or disassembly.
- Identify possible causes for the product's failure. Dismantle the product carefully, devising a system that allows it to be reassembled. For example, lay parts out carefully on a large flat surface, make annotated sketches or a digital photograph record.
- If the fault has been identified, try to repair the product and reassemble. When the product has been repaired, test it carefully (quality control). If the product is unwanted, could it be sold to raise funds for charity?
- If not, then separate parts for recycling or reuse in student projects.
- When students are designing and making their own electronic projects, encourage them to:
  - work in pairs to check each other's component handling and soldering skills
  - use components from irreparable products or unwanted projects
  - identify for themselves any faults in their circuits.

This will help encourage fault-finding and repair values. Think of the psychology and observe their response when they find the fault without the teacher's help.

Sustainable schools doorways

For more information visit:

www.wasteonline.org.uk
(electrical and electronic equipment recycling information)

Facelifts

How important is being fashionable?

Many products are discarded while they still work, because the surfaces of the product have become damaged or scratched, or because they have gone 'out of fashion' – they are the wrong colour,  or no longer convey the 'right messages' about the owner. Mobile phones, cameras, cycling helmets, bags, key rings and jewellery might all fit into this category.

Some designers have taken this problem on board, and replacement covers can now be purchased for iPods, mobile phones and Swatches.

Inspirational products

SMART cars can now be seen more often on our roads, and as a result the company's economic performance is improving. It was not always so, and the future of the Smart car was not always secure. The car was obviously designed to reduce the demand on road space and use less energy, but it is less well known that it is built at Smartville, a factory set up with sustainability in mind. The company monitors the ecological performance of both the factory and the product, and the modular design of the Smart car makes it easier to repair and ultimately recycle. However, its success has depended on its social acceptance as a fashionable form of transport, as well as its sound design principles.

Activities

- Discuss the products that you have recently thrown away. Did any of them still work? Could any of them have been given a facelift so that you would have kept them longer?

- Modularity is a design approach which makes updating for technical or visual reasons easier to do. Consider a range of common consumer products and sketch possibilities for their redesign in a modular way.

Make me last

- Choose a product that goes out of fashion and then redesign it so that its appearance can be easily changed. Show the product with a range of different styles conveying different images.

- Consider part of your school building that is in need of refurbishment. Redesign a refurbished version, and in such a way that it is easy to refurbish it 'next time'. Make a model showing the redesigned area.

Graphics

Sustainable schools
doorways

For more information see:

www.smart.com (details of the Smart sustainability policies can be found in 'ecology')

Encouraging repair

Can repaired clothes be cool?

Consumers in the UK spend on average £780 per person per year on textiles and clothing. That works out to be approximately 35 kg in textiles per person. Only one eighth of this is sent for reuse to charity shops and much of the rest is thrown away.

We could extend the life of clothes by repairing them, thereby stopping so much waste ending up in landfill.

Activities

Write a list of the clothes you or family members have bought in the past few years. If you've no longer got those clothes, what's happened to them and why have they been discarded? You might want to use headings:

- Clothes item
- Reason for discarding it
- Where's it gone?

How well have you done? Could any more of your clothes been reused by anyone?

Have any of your clothes been chucked out because they needed repairing?

What could retailers do to encourage people to repair clothes? What design feature would they have?

Ask older members in your family / community about how they used to repair clothes and any services that they used for clothes repair? See if they'll teach you a new skill! Do you think people used to repair more in the past? What has changed?

Make me last longer

- Set up a few focused tasks that enable students to repair textiles e.g. sew on a button, mend a seam.
- Set up a small enterprise activity by encouraging students to bring in some clothes that need repairing or fashion upgrading.
- Extension activity: Research the repair of textiles. There are some great sites that provide services for industrial and historical textiles being repaired.

Textiles

For more information, see:

www.unicor.gov/clothing_textiles (industrial repair of canvasses and uniforms)

www.caringfortextiles.com/ (historical textiles restoration)

www.quiltrepair.com (traditional American quilt repair)

Throw-away mentality

It's cheap, so why not throw it away?

Some things we get repaired when they break, or we repair them ourselves. Some things we do not repair – we throw them away.

This might be because they are beyond repair – or that it would cost too much – or that it is just easier to get a new one.

More sustainable design means...

- Designing for disassembly means that if a component fails it is easy to take the product apart and to replace or repair the dodgy component.
- There are many jobs in repairing products.
- Thrown-away products can end up causing pollution.

Many products are manufactured in Asian countries where labour is far cheaper than in Europe. But low-priced goods can contribute towards a throw-away mentality – and in turn this encourages design for throw-away. Use it once and bin it! But the new one will need more materials, more energy to make it and transport it, and will increase our footprint and contribute towards global warming and climate change.

Activity

Collect up some products
which are to be thrown away.
(Alternatively, make a list of
things that you never normally
repair or have repaired.)
Analyse them to see if they
can be better designed for
disassembly and repair.

RECYCLE

CALL BEFORE YOU DIG
REE LOCATIN

RECYCLE
Take an existing product that has become waste and re-process the material for use in a new product

Only part of the answer

Recycling is only a small bit of the answer...

Recycling, like reuse, prevents environmental damage linked to the production and processing of new materials. The process of recycling does, however, require energy for transportation and reprocessing.

Facts

- A recycled aluminium can saves enough energy to run a television for three hours.
- If all the aluminium cans in the UK were recycled there would be 14 million fewer full dustbins each year.
- There are over 2.5 billion cans recycled in the UK each year – that's equivalent to the weight of 18,000 double decker buses!

- Recycling one tonne of steel cans saves 1.5 tonnes of iron ore, 0.5 tonnes of coal and 40% of water usage.

Why recycling isn't enough

We're far better at recycling than we used to be – 22% of household waste was either recycled or composted in 2004/5 compared with only 6% ten years earlier. However, we are still generating more waste, so the total amount per person that goes into landfill is still high. Recycling isn't keeping up with the increase in waste we produce.

Statistics show that recycling makes very little difference to our eco-footprint. If we increased recycling by a further 20% we would reduce our footprint by 2%. If we managed the maximum 70% of stuff that can be recycled, we would still only reduce our footprint by 7%. So don't give up recycling, but remember it's only a small part of the answer!

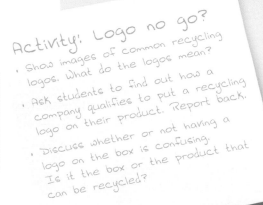

Activity: Logo no go?

- Show images of common recycling logos. What do the logos mean?
- Ask students to find out how a company qualifies to put a recycling logo on their product. Report back.
- Discuss whether or not having a logo on the box is confusing. Is it the box or the product that can be recycled?

Sustainability is not just about recycled paper, aluminium cans and plastic bottles. It's about redesigning everything in a more sustainable way.

For more information, see:

www.recycle-more.co.uk/

www.recycle-more.co.uk/nav/page632.aspx
(provides examples of recycling logos)

www.practicalaction.org/practicalanswers
(for a technical brief on recycling plastics)

Biodegradable packaging

Should food be packaged at all?

Most people associate recycling with food packaging: taking bottles to the bottle bank, washing out cans ready to be collected, saving milk cartons and aluminium cans for the recycling tip. We have all started to do something towards this sustainability issue, but is it enough?

More than half of all packaging is plastic, made from a non-renewable resource and the most difficult to recycle. Then there are mixed material packages such as Tetra Pak or Gualapack where recycling is even more difficult.

Product story

Tetra Pak is made up of 70% paperboard, 24% LDPE, a plastic, and 6% aluminium. It has been suggested that Tetra Paks can stop light depleting the vitamins and minerals in drinks, and that they are good because the paperboard is made from a renewable resource and is easy to recycle and transport.

At the moment, however, there is only one recycling plant in the UK for Tetra Pak cartons. On average, each household in the UK uses 2.3 kg of Tetra Pak cartons a year.

Product story

Belu now sell bottled water in a 'bio-bottle' made from corn starch that is composted back to soil in 12 weeks. They have not yet found a suitable material for the cap, so this needs to be recycled in the normal way. Innocent smoothies also use this type of bottle.

However, biodegradable tableware uses a greater weight of resources than ordinary disposable ones. (Vital Waste Graphics 2)

Activities

Get students to research biodegradable packaging such as potatopak and corn starch. Consider advantages and disadvantages of this type of packaging.

Get students to research all the different products in a supermarket that use Tetra Paks. Analyse this packaging. What is the nutritional value of the contents?

Eating leftover food can be classed as recycling as well as reusing, especially if it has been processed - made - into something different, e.g. croquettes. The other way to recycle food waste is to compost it. See the Reuse section for more on food leftovers.

Sustainable schools doorways

4

For more information, see:

www.drinkscartons.com
www.tetrapakrecycling.co.uk
www.belu.org
www.innocentdrinks.co.uk
www.vitalgraphics.net/waste/

Better use of batteries

What can we do with batteries?

Manufacture of a non-rechargeable battery requires five times the amount of energy it can deliver. Rechargeable batteries require less than twice the amount of energy to charge than they can deliver, and their lifespan is at least 500 charge/discharge cycles.

Of the 700 million batteries bought in the UK every year, 620 million are not rechargeable and 14 million are recycled. Told a different way,

we recycle 2% of non-rechargeable batteries and 5% of rechargeable batteries. The rest end up as household rubbish in landfill sites. This does not include vehicle batteries, which have a recycle rate of 90%, because they are collected at garages, scrapyards and civic amenity sites for recycling. Yet, there are schemes to recycle all batteries to reclaim metals such as cadmium, lead, and mercury, which are toxic, and nickel.

At the moment most batteries in the UK go to landfill sites with the general household waste, but the European Union has agreed the text of a law that will make recycling of batteries obligatory from 2008. The directive will ban most batteries with more than

a trace of the toxic chemicals cadmium or mercury. It says a quarter of all used batteries must be collected by 2012, rising to 45% by 2016 – and that at least half of them must be recycled.

Many countries in Europe already collect batteries, e.g. in 2002 Belgium collected 59%, Sweden 55%, Germany 39%, The Netherlands 32%, and France 16%.

Many of the non-rechargeable batteries that we throw away are not fully discharged, especially those from cameras and devices containing motors. This is because they have insufficient voltage to deliver the current to power the device. However, they could be used in low-current devices such as clocks and radios.

Activities

- Visit the Wasteonline website to find out more about types of battery and their reprocessing.

- Start a school scheme to collect unwanted batteries. Design a testing device to sort out batteries into those that have sufficient power remaining in them to power low current devices, such as clocks and radios, and those which do not ('flat'). Check if any batteries are rechargeable, and keep these separate. For safety reasons, do not attempt to recharge any of the batteries.

- Reuse the batteries that still have some life left: students could design and make their own clocks using the mechanisms commonly used in clock projects.

- To dispose of the batteries that are 'flat' find out about local recycling schemes. If a scheme exists then participate in it. If a scheme does not exist then start one and involve the civic council, local community and media. The Wasteonline website contains details of useful contacts. Produce an appropriate advertising campaign to raise awareness.

Sustainable schools
doorways

For more information, see:

www.wasteonline.org.uk
(battery recycling information)

What can be recycled?

Why don't we recycle more than we do?

Recycling is something that everyone says they would like to do and every local authority wants to see more of. Landfill taxes are going up and if we don't recycle more then Council Taxes will need to rise. So why don't we? What stops the people in your school, and in business, recycling more? One reason people give is that they are not sure what is possible, but it's quite easy to find out information now on the internet.

For example, the website www.recyclenow.com has a section telling what can be recycled and what cannot.

Facts

Everybody makes rubbish. Each week the average family in a developed country gets through 4 glass bottles or jars, 13 cans, 3 plastic bottles and 5 kilograms of paper. That means that every day a total of about 8,000 tonnes of rubbish is thrown away by families in England and Wales – that amount of rubbish is the same weight as 1,600 African elephants! (www.recycle-more.co.uk)

Inspirational product

Remarkable is a company that has taken a lead in producing products using recycled materials. The products range from pencils made from used vending cups, to books and mouse-mats from old car tyres. (www.remarkable.co.uk)

Activities

- Capture images of recycling opportunities, and create a poster showing all the materials that could be recycled in your school. Discuss why they are not all recycled (... if they're not!)

- Brainstorm interesting ways that the students, teachers and parents could be encouraged to recycle more, and sketch some storyboards showing the scenarios you have come up with.

- Recycling is just part of what it means to be a 'Sustainable School'. Find out what all the 'doorways' are and create a wall display to show them all, and how recycling fits in.

Make me easier to recycle

Design a recycling system for local or mass production for schools or for homes from recycled materials. The design should include ways of making the requirements and process of recycling easier to understand and carry out.

Graphics

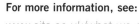

For more information, see:

www.sita.co.uk/what-we-do/recycling (general info on recycling materials)

www.recyclezone.org.uk (recycling)

www.inspirerecycle.org (inspiring products)

www.recoup.org (collecting and recycling plastics)

www.wastewatch.org.uk (waste generally)

www.wrap.org.uk (what's happening in UK)

www.education.gov.uk/search/results?q=sustainable+schools ('Sustainable schools')

Processes

What happens to old textiles?

A large amount of material goes to waste in the process of garment-making. Most of it is swept up and sent off to the nearest landfill – a waste of the energy and work that went into producing it.

Inspired product

Howies decided to make something out of all the cotton that was being wasted in the process of sweatshirt production. They now take all the cotton waste from the factory floors and recycle it. Interestingly, because it's a mix of all different grades of cotton, it gives the recycled cotton an irregular and washed-out look and feel (most companies use chemicals to achieve that look).

(www.howies.co.uk)

Activities

- Find out the eco-footprint of recycled materials compared with their first use. Look at www.beyond-waste.com/pdf/Ecofootprints.pdf and scroll down for facts on steel, plastic, glass, paper etc (pp 13-17). Work out the eco-footprint percentage you would save by using e.g. recycled glass compared with first use glass. Is it worth using recycled materials? Write a list of advantages for each one.

- Use a life cycle analysis to try to work out the processes and impacts of manufacturing a product from recycled materials, e.g. a recycled plastic picnic table. Use 'Where's the impact?' obtainable from CAT.

- Try the recycling game on www.lmb.co.uk

- Encourage students to find out about the processes involved in recycled fleece made from recycling plastic bottles. Is recycling bottles into fleece a good idea? What are the pros and cons?

- Check out textile recycling facilities near to where you live and find out about the organisations behind them.

Make me reusable

Have a go at mechanical recycling by unteasing woollen yarn and rewinding it with other woollen fibres.

For more information, see:

www.beyond-waste.com/pdf/Ecofootprints.pdf

www.wrap.org.uk/manufacturing/ info_by_material/index.html

www.wrap.org.uk/manufacturing/info_by_material?plastic?index.html

www.cat.org.uk

www.recyclenow.com
(recycling banks near your postcode)

www.stepin.org
(Case study on Patagonia fleeces)

www.patagonia.com

Recycle or reuse?

When is it appropriate to use recycled materials?

We should continue to use
recycled materials as much as we
can while they still exist, but we
should aim for a world where there
is less and less to recycle at all.

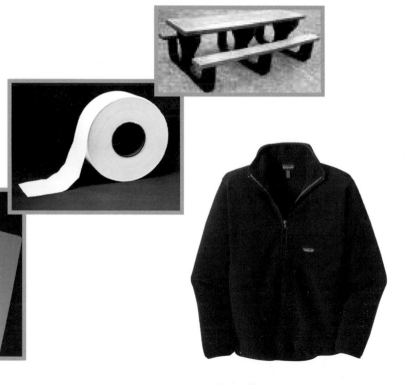

Activities

- Discuss the difference between reusing materials and recycling them. Why does recycling have a greater environmental impact than reuse?

- Find out the energy use of recycled materials compared with their first use. Look at www.beyond-waste.com/pdf/Ecofootprints.pdf and scroll down for facts on steel, plastic, glass, paper etc (pp 13-17). Work out the percentage of energy you would save by using e.g. recycled glass compared with first use glass. Is it worth using recycled materials? Write a list of advantages for each one.

- Investigate what you can use recycled materials for.

- Work out whether there are any recycled materials you could use in product design at school. Would it be beneficial and cost-effective? Are there any greater advantages for things that are bought for your home or school?

- Use a life cycle analysis to try to work out the processes and impacts of manufacturing a product from recycled materials, e.g. a recycled plastic picnic table made from the plastic film used for wrapping bales of hay. Use 'Where's the impact?' obtainable from CAT.

- Look at the definitions of 'REFUSE', 'REUSE' and 'RECYCLE'. If you had to choose between the three of them in terms of importance for a more sustainable world, which would you choose?

Sustainable schools
doorways

2 4

Links:

www.vitalgraphics.net/waste/
(see Vital Waste Graphics 2 p30-31)

www.wrap.org.uk/manufacturing.html
(details of all materials that can be recycled)

www.cat.org.uk/edresources

TOOLS

ECO-DESIGN TOOLS

Eco-Design Web

A method of evaluating any designing and making activity

Activity:
That's where I draw the line

This activity is to help students to evaluate their design ideas and products by comparing them against the original design criteria and suggest improvements.

- Before students begin a project, devise some sustainability criteria against which they can assess their completed project.

- When the project is completed, give out blank copies of the assessment sheet. (See p.160) Ask students to fill in the criteria along each line starting at 12 o'clock and working in a clockwise direction.

- Now ask them to assess their work according to the criteria, making an assessment from 1 to 10, where 10 is perfect and 1 is pretty awful. They should draw a coloured line the number of centimetres long that their assessment is.

- They also write an explanation of why they have given themselves the mark.

- They continue working in a clockwise direction in the same way for each of the criterion, except the last summative one.

- Before completing the last line, ask them to join the ends of each of their lines to make something like a web.

- Then make sure they think carefully about the last one, which should allow them to suggest how to make improvements. Ask them to consider how well they have done overall, then give themselves a mark, draw the line and complete the web.

- Finally, under their last line, they should suggest how they could have made improvements.

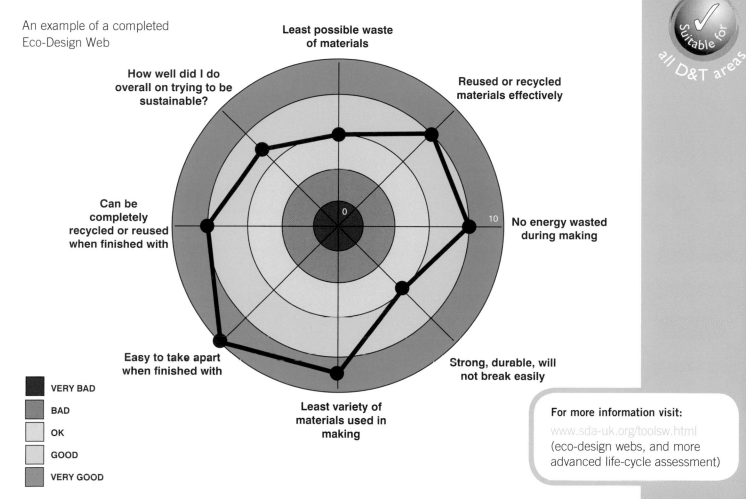

An example of a completed
Eco-Design Web

Least possible waste
of materials

How well did I do
overall on trying to be
sustainable?

Reused or recycled
materials effectively

Can be
completely
recycled or reused
when finished with

No energy wasted
during making

Easy to take apart
when finished with

Strong, durable, will
not break easily

Least variety of
materials used in
making

0

10

VERY BAD

BAD

OK

GOOD

VERY GOOD

For more information visit:
www.sda-uk.org/toolsw.html
(eco-design webs, and more
advanced life-cycle assessment)

Suitable for
all D&T areas

Design Abacus

A method by which students can evaluate the sustainability of a product, compare two products, or evaluate their own products

Activity: Product evaluation

- Decide on the type of assessment you want your students to consider - life cycle, environmental issues, economic issues, social issues, etc.
- Develop a set of criteria for them to use, either in advance or with the class.
- Work on one or two criteria with the class to give them the idea.
- For each criterion, ask students to assess the product/s on a scale of +2 (very good) to -2 (very poor) and mark on the abacus.
- Also ask them to consider their confidence in their assessment and to mark it on the abacus as low, medium or high. They might just guess, which is fine.
- Complete assessments for all criteria and join them up as shown.
- To compare two products, repeat the process in a different colour.
- Students can now research areas where their confidence is low.
- They can also identify elements of existing products they might want to include in their own designs to make them more sustainable.
- Re-design They could also discuss ways in which the product could be re-designed to make it more sustainable.

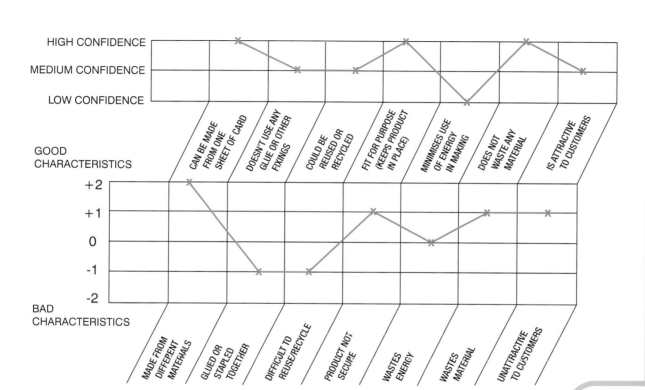

HIGH CONFIDENCE
MEDIUM CONFIDENCE
LOW CONFIDENCE

GOOD
CHARACTERISTICS

+2
+1
0
-1
-2

BAD
CHARACTERISTICS

CAN BE MADE FROM ONE SHEET OF CARD
DOESN'T USE ANY GLUE OR OTHER FIXINGS
COULD BE REUSED OR RECYCLED
FIT FOR PURPOSE (KEEPS PRODUCT IN PLACE)
MINIMISES USE OF ENERGY IN MAKING
DOES NOT WASTE ANY MATERIAL
IS ATTRACTIVE TO CUSTOMERS

MADE FROM DIFFERENT MATERIALS
GLUED OR STAPLED TOGETHER
DIFFICULT TO REUSE/RECYCLE
PRODUCT NOT SECURE
WASTES ENERGY
WASTES MATERIAL
UNATTRACTIVE TO CUSTOMERS

FOCAL AREA

PACKAGING

Adaptation of Integrated Design abacus, Shot in the Dark, 2000

Suitable for all D&T areas

For more information visit:
www.sda-uk.org/toolsa.html
(more advanced life-cycle
assessment)

Eco-Design Web template

How well did I do overall on trying to be sustainable?

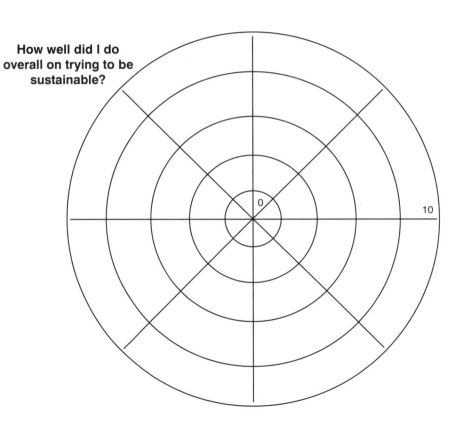

0

10

Design Abacus template

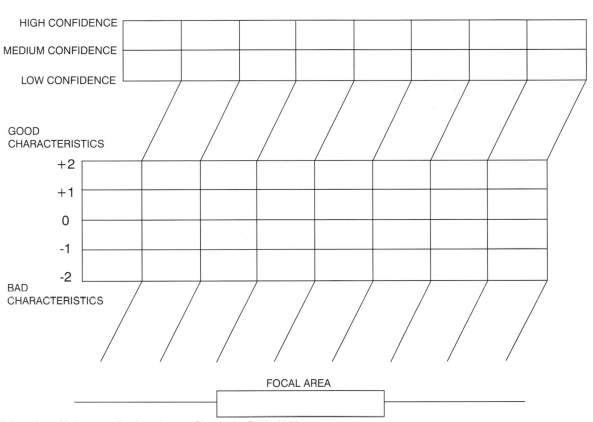

HIGH CONFIDENCE

MEDIUM CONFIDENCE

LOW CONFIDENCE

GOOD
CHARACTERISTICS

+2

+1

0

-1

-2

BAD
CHARACTERISTICS

FOCAL AREA

Adaptation of Integrated Design abacus, Shot in the Dark, 2000

Winners and Losers

Product impact on people

Purpose of the task: to evaluate a product's impact and/or to compare the impact of similar products.

You will need: circles charts (opposite), product(s) or product case study, colouring pencils.

Every product affects **people** at different stages of the product life cycle: for example, people are involved in designing, making, using and disposing of the product.

Activity

Get the students into groups of three/four. Students write the name of the product(s) in the centre circle on the sheet, for example fair trade T-shirt and non-fair trade T-shirt (if comparing two products).

On the chart

Take one product. In the segments around the centre circle, write down the people/groups who are involved and affected by the product at different stages of the product life cycle. Use a segment per person affected. For example designer, manufacturer, user, rubbish collector.

You may find it useful to use the following questions to fill in the outer segments. Does the product

· improve the quality of life for its users?

· infringe basic rights of people involved in manufacturing e.g. fair wages, decent working conditions?

· encourage us to enjoy the company of others?

Look at the list of people affected

· Which of those people benefit? Now colour them in green.

· Which of those people lose out? Colour them in red.

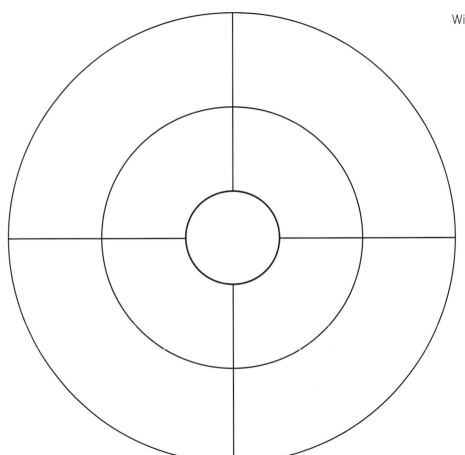

Winners & Losers Template

Remember – there are often no right or wrong answers – each person may have different views on whether a product is having a good or bad impact!

For more information visit:

www.sda-uk.org?SUSTAINABILITY%20SECTION/social.htm
(for more ideas of questions on social impacts)

www.nosweat.org.uk and www.ethicaltrade.org, www.corporatewatch.org.uk
(for background research on issues people involved in manufacturing)

Where to find more information

PRACTICAL ACTION

Schools Department
Practical Action
The Schumacher Centre
Bourton on Dunsmore
Rugby, Warwickshire, CV23 9QZ
01926 634400
Email:schools@practicalaction.org.uk
www.practicalaction.org/schools

Biothinking

Edwin Datschefski
01883 650 238
www.biothinking.com

Centre for Alternative Technology

Machynlleth
Powys SY20 9AZ
01654 705963 (education)
01654 705 993 (shop)
www.cat.org.uk/edresources

Friends of the Earth

26-28 Underwood Street, London N1 7JQ
020 7490 1555
www.foe.org.uk

Howies

Howies Ltd
Bath House Road, Cardigan, SA43 1JY
01329 614 122
www.howies.org.uk

Labour behind the Label

38 Exchange Street
Norwich NR2 1AX
01603 666160
www.labourbehindthelabel.org

People Tree

People Tree Ltd
Studio 7
8-13 New Inn Street, London EC2A 3PY
0 20 7739 0660
E-mail people@peopletree.co.uk
www.peopletree.co.uk

Soil Association

Bristol House
40-56 Victoria Street,Bristol BS1 6BY
0117 314 5000
E-mail info@soilassocaition.org
www.soilassociation.org

SUSTRANS

2 Cathedral Square
College Green, Bristol BS1 5DD
0117 926 8893
www.sustrans.com

Traidcraft

Kingsway, Gateshead
Tyne and Wear NE11 ONE
0191 491 0591
www.traidcraft.co.uk

Oxfam

Oxfam Education
Oxfam House
John Smith Drive, Oxford OX4 3JY
www.oxfam.org.uk/education

MORE...

Practical Action in Schools

PRACTICAL ACTION

Schools Department
Practical Action
The Schumacher Centre
Bourton on Dunsmore
Rugby, Warwickshire, CV23 9QZ
01926 634400

Email:schools@practicalaction.org.uk

Practical Action in Schools

For information on our free downloadable resources, www.practicalaction.org/schools

For Practical Action's printed publications for schools, visit www.developmentbookshop.com

Sustainability Matters in Design and Technology

The pack contains a CD with six presentations covering each Design and technology material area, linked with teachers' notes and photocopiable sheets for students on themes of sustainable designers, dimensions of sustainability and the Six R's.

CD Pack, 12 postcards
ISBN 978 1 85339 708 0

Wall to Wall Design (key stage 3)

Focuses on the cultural and environmental issues involved in building new homes in Kenya and the UK and includes activity sheets to help students apply their understanding of sustainable approaches to design.

48 pages, plus two posters; ISBN 1 85339 513 7

Sustainable Lifestyles? (key stage 4)

Exploring economic and cultural issues in Design and Technology this pack is designed to tackle complex economic and cultural issues associated with sustainable technologies. It includes a wide range of focused tasks and DMAs appropriate for all focus areas.

A4 ring binder, photocopiable worksheets, case studies and poster, 133 pages; ISBN 1 85339 548

Hands On Technology
(key stage 4)

This video package presents real-life examples of successful sustainable technology stories. It contains case studies in three focus areas – product design, food technology and textiles technology – and is supported by teachers' notes and student activities.

A4 ring binder, photocopiable activity sheets and guidance notes for teachers, 58 page guide; ISBN 1 85339 5870

In a Nutshell
(key stage 4)

The pack promotes an understanding of cultural, environmental and economic dimensions of sustainability. It contains information about food processing and small-scale industry by using case studies of peanut butter production in Zimbabwe.

10 work cards, poster guide for teachers, 16 pages; ISBN 1 85339 5498

Development @ IT
(key stage 4 and post 16)

This full-colour booklet gives an introduction to development and the part that appropriate technology can play in improving people's lives. It begins by investigating the meaning of development and exploring the reasons for the development gap.

16 pages

Order any of these resources at www.developmentbookshop.com

CAT's EDUCATION RESOURCES

CAT pupils' guides to renewable energy provide background information suitable for Key stage 3 and 4 pupils. The three guides cover solar power, water power, and wind power.

CAT teacher's guide to renewable energy provide practical information on how to help pupils achieve success with working models, mostly on a small scale, useful to teachers at any level from Key stage 1 to post-16. There are four guides, covering solar power (electricity projects), solar power (heating projects), wind power, and water power.

Where's the Impact?
(KS2 to post-16)

Contains:
- an introduction to Ecological Footprinting

- photocopiable sheets to produce cards for the activity

- photocopiable extension activity cards on energy, recycled resources, transport and global issues

- sources of further information.

Pupils' and Teachers' Guides available as downloads at www.cat.org.uk/catpubs

Where's the Impact? **available in hard copy or as download at www.cat.org.uk/edresources**

Acknowledgements

Pack co-ordinator:
Ian Capewell (Practical Action)

Writers:
Ian Capewell, Cathryn Gathercole,
Bren Hellier *(Practical Action)*

Rhoda Trimingham, Eddie
Norman, Peter Simmons, Nigel
Zanker *(Loughborough University)*

Ann Macgarry, Jo Gwillim
(Centre for Alternative Technology)

Lesley Woods *(Food
technology teacher)*

James Pitt *(The University of York)*

Contributors:
Design and Technology PGCE
students *(Loughborough
University)* 2006-07

Design and technology teachers:
Kevin Hull, Clare Cooper, Liz
Cook, Brian Hurlow, Jill Shepherd,
Catherine Murphy, Russ Harris,
Mary Southall, Carol Sutcliffe, Mike
Beloe, Cathy Growney, Kim Kenny,
Donna Trebell, Mark Wilders.

Initial pack design:
Peter Simmons, Rhoda
Trimingham, Shayal Chhibber and
Gina Tomlinson *(Loughborough
University).*

Editor: Kim Daniel

Designer: Renaissance Creative

Translator: Ceri Tomos

**With thanks to the following
organisations for their support:**
The Design and Technology
Association (DATA).

Funders: European Community,
Countryside Commission for Wales.

Images and product stories:
Howies, People Tree, Cerys Marks,
Remarkable, TRAID Remade,
Labour Behind the Label, Oxfam,
Practical Action, Centre for
Alternative Technology, Laurie Pitt.

Practical Action is the working name of Intermediate Technology Development Group Ltd
The Schumacher Centre, Bourton on Dunsmore, Rugby, Warwickshire, CV23 9QZ, UK.
Company Reg. No. 871954, England I Reg. Charity No. 247257